NEVER TRY TO DRINK A CHINESE WOMAN UNDER THE TABLE

Plus Other Fun and Practical Tips for Doing Business in China and at Home

D1617047

RICHARD BRADSPIES & J.D. FOX

You understand us better than we understand ourselves.
"Mr. S" (a high-ranking Chinese business executive,
who insists on anonymity for his personal protection).

What if you want a grilled cheese sandwich for lunch but you're
served braised frogs with tofu in spiced chili broth? "Never Try to
Drink A Chinese Woman Under the Table" is a funny, entertaining and
indispensable guide that will help Americans avoid culture shock and
shame when living, shopping, eating or doing business with Asians.
Susan Shapiro, author of "Only as Good as Your Word" and "The Bosnia
List"

The Chinese are justifiably proud of their culture and heritage, and their
traditions inform the way they do business. "Never Try" lets Westerners
in on the secrets.
Bill Black, Global China Practice Leader
Fleishman Hillard Worldwide Public Affairs

"Never Try" is a breakthrough volume on how to survive and thrive within
the Chinese business environment. Well written and at times hysterically
funny, this book is a must read for everyone from the occasional tourist
to the old time "China Hands." If you have even a feint interest in
approaching the Chinese market, this is the book you should read first.
Bill Schmick, Berkshire Money Management portfolio manager,
international investing pioneer, and syndicated columnist.
Blog:afewdollarsmore.com

"Never Try" has a lofty goal -- through cultural understanding, we can
make the world a smaller and more civil place. The authors not only hit
the mark, but do it with such good humor!
Mary Civiello, Emmy-winning TV journalist, executive media coach,
Author, "Communication Counts: Business Presentations for Busy
People"

Who lost China? If you read this book, and take to heart its message, no
one will be able to accuse you of being the one who dropped the ball on
the China account. Richard Bradspies and J.D. Fox have stuffed this book
full of practical advice, amusingly conveyed, with case studies to show
you how you can successfully do business with the Chinese -- and have
fun, too!
John DeDakis, former Senior Editor, CNN's "The Situation Room with
Wolf Blitzer"
Author, "Troubled Water"

The authors humorously demystify every aspect of business and personal behavior in this ancient culture—which in many ways is more modern than most Westerners think. While some traditions continue, new ones are taking their place that keep the Chinese mystique and economic miracle alive. Readers will enjoy learning new traditions in an entertaining way and how to practice old traditions the correct way.
Professor Robert F. Noltenmeier, New York University (NYU)

Teaching Chinese students in China was like drinking from a cultural fire hose! Sure, I'd had Chinese students in my English classes before, but then during a cultural exchange program I was sent to their turf – and it was truly a different world.   I wish I'd had the chance to read "Never Try" before I had to spend all that time trying!
Jeff Eldot, English as a Second Language (ESL) Program Director
Phoenix College, Phoenix, Arizona

From Both of Us:
Our thanks to Barbara Casey, our amazing agent, whose unwavering belief in our book made it possible. And, to our publishers at Strategic Media Books for taking a chance on us.

From Rich:
To my Chinese colleagues and friends, who suggested that I write this book, and over more than 11 years shared adventures and travels. Thank you for everything.

From J.D.:
To my teachers, students, friends and family. Nothing good happens without help and support.

TABLE OF CONTENTS

INTRODUCTION

PART ONE – Blending In:
What to Expect OUTSIDE the Office

FOOD:
Duck Blood Soup. Seriously?

ALCOHOL:
Americans are Amateurs, the Chinese Have Gone Pro

SEX:
Do It, But Don't Discuss It

PART TWO – Your Chinese Colleagues:
How They Think, Why They Keep to Themselves,
How That's Changing

GENERATIONAL CHANGE:
The Aging Revolutionaries,
The Questioning Middle,
The Start-Ups

NAME-BRAND STATUS:
Let's Go Shopping!

LOSS OF FACE:
Where Did It Go?

BIG NOSE:
More Than How You Look

LANGUAGE:
You Have a Choice (or Two)

FEAR OF FLIGHT:
The Passport Paradox

GOING SOLO VERSUS GROUP THINK:
Americans are Lone Wolves,
The Chinese are Pack Animals

PART THREE – The Corporate Environment:
What to Expect INSIDE the Office

CLIMBING THE LADDER:
How High Can You Go?

WHO'S TO BLAME?
The Art of Consensus

THE OFFICE RUMOR MILL
The Real Information Superhighway

PERFORMANCE APPRAISALS:
Better to Be an Idiot Than 10 Seconds Late

WHEN DOES "YES"
Actually Mean Yes?

FOCUS:
Just Give Us What We Want!

PUTTING IT TOGETHER:
Telling You What We Told You

BONUS:
Your Maiden Voyage to China

About the Authors

9

What We Want You to Learn; How We Teach

CAUTION:

We're Going to Have Fun. Prepare to Lighten Up!

HERE'S HOW RICHARD learned that Asians operate very distinctly when doing business: at his first interview with the head of a Chinese company, he was asked if he wanted a glass of water. What turned up was a glass of HOT water. The Chinese don't generally drink cold water – they think it's unhealthy. Who knew?

For anyone interested in doing business with the Chinese and other Asians, we want to help make the road a little less bumpy. We'll show you when your American business experience might prove useful, and where it may lead you down the wrong road and you need to take an alternate route.

Our primary focus is the Chinese way of doing business. We're going to cover a wide variety of topics. In each, consistent with the way it's probably taught in business school (if it's taught at all), we're going to lay out the topic, then demonstrate in a real world case study what you might face. We'll review the top lessons you should learn. Finally, we'll offer a sidebar on the topic as it relates to other Asian businesspeople and their respective cultures.

A few quick notes before we get started:

- A lot of what's being presented has to do with cultural differences, reflecting Chinese history and practice.

- Just because the Chinese do things differently, it doesn't mean their way is wrong. If you take away only one lesson from this book, here it is: as Americans, we don't know better. We know different. To survive and thrive when doing business with the Chinese, that has to be in the forefront of your mind.

- This is important stuff, but we mean to have fun with it. C'mon, a business culture featuring banquets where people drink fortified rice wine until they pass out, their stomachs full of duck tongues with Sichuan peppercorns? How can you not have fun with that?

Blending In:

What to Expect OUTSIDE the Office

FOOD

Duck Blood Soup. Seriously?

IF YOU CONSIDER DINING an adventure, you'll love doing business with the Chinese. But, if your idea of an exotic meal is slapping a tomato on your toasted cheese sandwich, sit down. Your dining experience is about to change. Doing business with the Chinese means a walk on the wild side of the culinary arts. Here are just 10 of the foods you may encounter:

1. Ox tongue & tripe with roasted chili-peanut vinaigrette
2. Diced rabbit & peanuts with chili-garlic black beans
3. Duck tongues with Sichuan peppercorns
4. Jellyfish with scallion sesame oil
5. Mung bean jello with chili miso black bean sauce
6. Braised frogs with napa, bamboo, tofu in spiced chili broth
7. Braised sea cucumber with shiitake mushrooms & bamboo shoots
8. Stir-fried intestines

9. Duck blood soup
10. Barbequed giant insects on skewers

Okay, to be honest, you're going to run into more than 10 foods you've never eaten before. How about an additional five? [Trust us; there are many more.]

1. Beef lungs in chili sauce
2. Ox stomach in garlic sauce
3. Sautéed pig's kidney
4. Braised ox stomach and pork blood in spicy soup
5. Wood ear mushrooms in vinegar sauce

If you're already holding your stomach, we feel your pain. Maybe you're not cut out for doing business with the Chinese, and should return this book right now. Why does it matter, and why do we start on the topic of food?

Hey, you gotta eat – and with the Chinese, it's more than a meal.

Yes, you do have to eat. But there's more to it than that. Doing business with the Chinese revolves around food. Their food, eaten with chopsticks. Based on countless meals endured and even enjoyed (we're adventurous eaters) here's what you need to know:

- Food is of critical importance to the Chinese. Sharing food together is even more important.

- Unless you have something that the Chinese desperately need and absolutely cannot get anywhere else, you cannot expect to close a deal in the office. People get to know each other over food (and over drink too, but more on that later). Trust gets built over meals.

- Banquets are an important part of the Chinese culture and are at the center of doing business. You get to know your business partners over many evenings of shared food and drinks. To the non-Chinese, many of the dishes served will be unfamiliar and strange. It might seem unimaginable that you will have to even take one small taste. But taste you must, if you want to be considered for the business deal. As the weird dishes keep coming, it becomes an endurance contest to see whether you can get the congealed duck blood down your throat without gagging, or even worse. Keep smiling! If you do, you will rack up bonus points, and the Chinese keep score.

- When the Chinese go out for a restaurant meal, deciding what to eat is a long and involved process. Unless the food is pre-ordered for a banquet, there is a slow dance with the waiter in deciding what to order. The waiter will be quizzed on his culinary knowledge. It is not unusual to spend 10 or 15 minutes talking about how each dish is prepared, what ingredients are used, and whether the fish is really fresh. Of course, you won't participate in these decisions, since they'll all take place in Mandarin. And besides, what do you know about authentic Chinese food?

- Deal breaker: unlike in the United States, no one ever chooses their own food. Everyone eats communally. If you can't bear the idea of sharing your meals, then don't plan on doing business with the Chinese, even in the United States, because the food rules are the same.

- As dishes are placed on the table, never serve yourself. You will always be the honored guest, sitting beside the host, who is always the senior person in the group. He (sometimes she) will serve you first. Dishes are served one at a time – no combination plates in China! Later in the meal, after you have been served, it is polite for you to then serve your host seconds, as well as refill his tea cup.

- There is a strict code to follow, and if you serve yourself, you are being disrespectful to your hosts (more about that later in our chapter "Loss of Face").

- Meals are long, relaxed events but there is a set choreography. At banquets, it is common to have 10 or 12 courses. When the whole fish comes out, you can breathe a long sigh of relief – the meal is coming to a close. You aren't there yet, but the end is in sight. A whole fish (as well as other prestige dishes such as birds nest and abalone) are symbols of wealth, and generosity. After the fish course, there is typically a rice or noodle course (it depends on the province of China you are in whether you will be served rice or noodles). Then comes dessert.

- The Chinese do not have a sweet tooth like Americans do. No chocolate molten cake. No mousse. No ice cream sundaes. Desserts are generally just a large platter of fresh fruits. At banquets, there will be at least one other dessert before the fruit. Often a sweet soup with sesame dumplings will be served.

- When you serve someone food or drink, watch for them to tap their first two fingers on the table, in succession three or four times, which means: "thank you for your kindness; you've served me enough." This happens at every type of meal, whether it's two people having lunch together, or a banquet. Of course, you should also tap your fingers when someone serves you.

- Teacups do not have handles, and tea is served extra hot. Caution is required to avoid burning your fingers, or dropping the cup. You can always wait a bit for the tea to cool.

CASE STUDY

Let's put it all together with our buddy Tom from Indiana, who sells grain for a midsized company. Tom has seen the numbers, and knows how vast a market the Chinese offer for his product. He's been deputized as the leader of his company's effort to break into the Chinese market.

Tom takes his first trip to the other side of the world. He arrives in Beijing the night before his scheduled day of meetings with a potential Chinese customer. He didn't know what jet lag was until now. He's able to get something to eat from a Pizza Hut, but isn't sure if he should eat the sausage pizza he ordered. It sure doesn't look like Indiana Pizza Hut. It looks more like someone stuck frankfurters on top of a pizza, then added some bizarre spices that Tom has never smelled or tasted before.

After Tom calls his family and gets a few hours of sleep, he's in for a continuous day of meetings at his potential Chinese partner's headquarters. He will meet with four senior executives in the company over the course of a single day.

The meetings go well. Tom becomes more relaxed, because he gets a lot of positive affirmation from his hosts (but Tom will later learn that a roomful of people nodding and smiling doesn't necessarily mean approval – see our chapter "When Does Yes Mean Yes?"). He doesn't understand a word of Mandarin, but the executive translating for him, let's call him Mr. Shu, is terrific. The Chinese are very cordial, as he heard they would be. They've even invited him to dinner that evening. Tom has been heading sales teams on the other side of the world for years, and feels in his bones that he's striking gold with every step he takes.

The Chinese eat early. The banquet, in Tom's honor, is set for 6 p.m. That gives him enough time for a quick nap back at his hotel. The car to deliver Tom to his first authentic Chinese meal is precisely on time, and by now he's used to the rush at the car door whenever an automobile approaches the hotel entrance – hawkers open the door and throw in cards advertising the "massage services" of scantily-clad women. Tom focuses instead on the food: he has always loved Chicken Chow Mein in his suburban Indiana neighborhood, and can only imagine how much better it will be in Beijing!

The restaurant is huge. Mr. Shu ushers Tom past tables with seating for hundreds and palatial decorations overhead. But Tom won't be sitting in the warehouse-sized main room. They go down a long corridor with a series of private banquet rooms. At his host's elite level, they would never consider eating with the masses.

The banquet room looks like a giant living/dining room back home. There's a large flat screen television tuned to a Chinese soap opera (Tom doesn't understand a word of it, but the actors are attractive), couches and padded chairs around the perimeter, and a large dining table set for 12.

Tom looks for the bar. He'd love a sturdy cocktail after his long day. No luck. He's guided to the sofa, sits down, and is immediately given a small cup of hot green tea (with no sugar). Tom is a coffee guy; and has never tasted green tea. It's (we can't resist) not his cup of tea. He sips it slowly, hoping for the liquid relief of a martini.

The four people he met with during the day are there, and seven other company executives show up. Aside from Mr. Shu, no one speaks English to him. Introductions are made, business cards are exchanged, and he's suddenly lost in a room where Mandarin is being spoken and he doesn't understand a word. Mr. Shu occasionally smiles, but has stopped translating every word for Tom. It's unsettling. Tom doesn't know how much of the conversation is about him and the impression he made during the day's meetings. And still no martini.

Tom smiles whenever he's smiled at, but his thoughts drift to food, and the wonderful meal he knows is ahead. He's built up an appetite after a long day in the office. Along with his Chicken Chow Mein, he plans to also order wonton soup and fried rice.

While he's thinking about the meal, everyone moves toward the table. He's politely ushered to a seat next to the company's president. Mr. Shu, Tom's only English-speaking acquaintance, mercifully takes the seat on Tom's other side.

Everyone else sits, and very quickly a large platter of food is brought to the table. The platter is placed in front of the president, who picks up chopsticks, and starts putting food onto Tom's plate. The platter moves swiftly around the table, everyone else getting served in turn. The other 11 people in the room start to eat as soon as food is placed in front of them.

There's no fork for Tom, and he doesn't know how to use chopsticks. He watches everyone else using them, and figures he can too. He looks down at his plate: orange gunk, thin slices of brown material, slivers of some kind of vegetable – he has no clue.

Tom deftly decides to go for the thin slices of what look like meat, picks up his chopstick, manages to get ahold of a single piece, and watches it fall into his lap. He hopes no one has seen this, makes a second attempt, which makes it to his mouth. It's cold beef, and tastes good.

One of the hosts sees his difficulties, and miraculously a fork and knife appear. [Note: Chinese restaurants, upon sighting Americans, may automatically bring out silverware for them.] He asks Mr. Shu what is on his plate. The orange gunk is jellyfish. The thin slices of cold meat are actually beef tendon. He knows what the cucumber-looking vegetable is – cucumber. He tries it, and leaves the gunky jellyfish alone.

Tom feels a little better now that he's got a fork, and starts to think of himself as an adventurous diner. He looks for a waiter with menus.

Menus never arrive. The plates are cleared away, and a cart is rolled in, with an entire crispy Peking duck laid out. The waiter takes out a giant hatchet, and begins to expertly carve the duck into very thin slices. They're placed on thin pancakes with cucumber scallions and brushed with hoisin sauce. They look sort of like the burritos Tom occasionally enjoyed at the Mexican restaurant back home. He notices that some of his dinner partners are using chopsticks to pick up the wraps, while others are using their hands. Tom grabs his, and has his first take of authentic Peking duck. He likes it!

Tom's confidence begins to rebuild. Even though he doesn't understand the language and is still jet-lagged, he can handle the food!

Scallops with broccoli come next on a platter. The company's president serves Tom first, and then the platter goes around the table. Tom, remembering the earlier passed dish, starts eating right away with his knife and fork. This dish is tasty, but he'd like rice too. That's the way he's used to eating Chinese food. But there's none on the table, and no one asks for it.

The next dish looks and tastes like spicy chicken, and again Tom likes the taste – could this be authentic Kung Pao Chicken? Well, no. Mr. Shu chuckles and tells him it's rabbit. Specifically, diced rabbit in peanuts. Tom makes a mental note to not tell his kids that he just ate the Easter Bunny.

The next dish is sliced, slimy, greyish-green, and bland. Tom tastes, but doesn't eat it. Good call, Tom. Sea cucumber isn't for the faint of heart, but you get points for trying.

Next up, unbeknownst to Tom, is sautéed pig's kidney. It looks like a blown-up turkey kidney from an American Thanksgiving feast, but is served in a thick viscous brown sauce with a unique (nasty) smell. Tom passes on even tasting this one. He starts wondering if there might be a tactful way to exit, go back to his hotel, and order a burger and fries from room service. But they don't speak much English at his hotel, and Tom doesn't want another adventure similar to the Chinese-spiced frankfurter and tomato bread from Pizza Hut.

Tom's food daydream is interrupted by the arrival of a vegetable he's never seen before. It looks like a cross between a cucumber and squash, served with mushrooms. Tom takes a bite. It's crunchy, with a bitter taste that's odd but slightly appealing. It's bitter melon – long, gourd-like, and supposed to enhance health (like many Chinese foods). Mr. Shu nods approvingly at Tom's effort.

For his part, Tom is wondering how many more platters of strange food are coming when the waiters lug in a humungous steamed fish with head and tail. Since he's the guest of honor, the president carves off a slice of fish cheek, a small filet of the fleshy body, and then gouges out one eye. All three are delicately and proudly placed on Tom's plate. Tom eats the filet, struggles with the cheek, and doesn't even make an attempt at the eye. Mr. Shu looks down.

Still more to come. Rice with bits of eggs, shrimp, and pork. Young chow fried rice. Tasty, and familiar to American palates. Tom likes it. Then, warm red bean soup – sweet, with sort of a yellowish red color.

Finally, a big platter of mixed fruit. Watermelon, orange sections and cherry tomatoes, served together. Goofy, Tom thinks, but edible.

There's a lazy Susan on the middle of the table, where all the leftovers have been placed. The 11 others in the room start to pick at the plates. Tom just counts the number of dishes he was able to eat, the number he couldn't, and resolves to thank his wife for each and every meal she prepares from now on.

Tom has survived his first Chinese meal. He definitely came off as an inexperienced American by stumbling with his chopsticks, and wouldn't eat the more exotic dishes, but he got a few points for hanging in through the meal.

FOOD LESSONS

So, would it have helped Tom to know the lay of the land before he got to China? We think so. Let's review.

1. Food is an extremely important part of the Chinese culture, and you cannot close a deal without building trust over food.
2. If you don't have an adventurous sense of dining, it's going to be difficult to do business in China. The more open you are to trying new dishes, or at least enthusiastically fake enjoying them, the more bonus points you will earn.
3. As a foreigner, you are always the honored guest, and will be seated next to the host (the most senior person in the dining group).
4. Menus are never presented, and you don't select individual dishes.
5. Dishes are served sequentially, one at a time.
6. Never serve yourself (for the first serving of each course; you can pick off the LAZY SUSAN later).
7. Learn how to use chopsticks.
8. If you absolutely cannot learn how to use chopsticks (really, try hard), ask for a knife and fork.
9. It's the host's role to serve the guest, and loss of face for the host is immediate if you serve yourself – an unpardonable sin.
10. For the Chinese, business banquets are a perk – free food and drink – plus a chance to socialize with their colleagues.

SIDEBAR:
Authentic Asian Food Beyond China

Our expertise is China, but of course we know that the world's other economic superpower is one of just 52 countries in Asia. Each one has its own cultural traditions, customs, and food.

On this front, we need your help. We want to understand – and help our readers understand – the different foods one might encounter in countries throughout Asia (and the foods one might face in America when doing business with colleagues from other Asian countries).

We welcome your comments and suggestions on our blog. Here's the address:

Never Try to Drink a Chinese Woman Under the Table
[Plus Other Fun and Practical Tips]
www.nevertrythis.net

To get you started, we did a little research, and came up with a list for five of the other Asian countries with their own notable cuisine and unique dishes.

Take a look (and you thought China required a strong, adventurous stomach!):

JAPAN

1. Deadly Blowfish
2. Fish Sperm
3. Raw Horse Meat
4. Aquatic Insects
5. Fermented Seafood
6. Octopus Ice Cream
7. Canned Bread
8. Placenta Jelly Drink
9. Wasp Crackers
10. Hairy Seaweed

PHILIPPINES

1. Blood Stew
2. Fried Crickets in Soy Sauce
3. Crispy Pigs Feet
4. Dog Meat Stew
5. Sizzling Pigs Head
6. Beaten to Death Chicken
7. Chicken Intestines
8. Crunchy Fried Small Fish
9. Battered and Fried Pregnant Fish
10. Boiled Duck Embryo

SOUTH KOREA

1. Live Seafood Soup
2. Acorn Jelly
3. Fermented Skate
4. Dead Body Soup
5. Boiled Intestine Sausage
6. Barbequed Intestines
7. Steamed Silkworm Larvae
8. Live Octopus
9. Dog Stew
10. Live Spoon Worms

INDONESIA

1. Smoked Bats
2. Monkey Toes
3. Cold Dog Sate
4. Fried Chicken Head
5. Tiny Baby Birds
6. Cobra
7. Black Dog Meat
8. Forest Rat With White Tail
9. Black Snake
10. Poo-Eating Shellfish

THAILAND

1. Bloody Pork Sour and Spicy Salad
2. Dancing (Live) Shrimp
3. Ants Eggs
4. Dull Red Raw Beef With Extra Blood and Mint

5. Salted Duck Red Egg Yolk
6. Red Ant Salad
7. Rat Salad
8. Papaya Salad with Fermented Shrimp or Mussels
9. Onion Fried Frog
10. Centipede on a Stick

Got more, got corrections, or got a list from another Asian country? Tell us about it on our blog! We also welcome recipes and tips for surviving (or even enjoying) these foods.

Now, before we go on, we want to preemptively answer any critics who think we're picking on Asian countries for their culinary distinctiveness. Remember, we are Americans with a sense of fair play – as long as it's coupled with laughter. So, we end with the flip side, namely:

American Foods That Make Many Foreigners Gag
1. Biscuits and Gravy
2. Bacon and Eggs
3. Peanut Butter
4. Soft Bread
5. Mayonnaise
6. Grits
7. Fluffer Nutter Sandwiches
8. Chicken Fried Steak with Cream Gravy
9. Deep Fried Snickers Bars
10. Huge Portions at All-You-Can-Eat Buffets

NEVER TRY TO DRINK A CHINESE WOMAN UNDER THE TABLE

ALCOHOL

Americans are Amateurs. The Chinese Have Gone Pro

WE BEGIN WITH A CONFESSION. The first chapter on food didn't tell you everything you need to know. We just didn't have the heart to lay the intricacies of the Chinese banquet on you in one shot, so we cut the story in half. First, just the food.

Now, the food's complement: the drink. You know we aren't talking green tea here. Alcohol. Lots and lots of it. Sometimes it will taste great (when you're drinking fine French Bordeaux and Champagne). More often, it will be fortified rice wine, called Wu Liang Ye (woo lee ang yee). Some people actually like it; others think you could switch it out with the antifreeze in your car.

China has also become a major wine producer. The brand you will most often see is "Great Wall." Much of it is thin and boring but the high-end red wine is surprisingly world class.

Here's what you need to know:

- The Chinese drink like American college students: they drink to get drunk, and get drunk as fast as they can. They don't sip fine wine, they guzzle it. Whatever the drink of choice, they take it down like a shot.

- The Chinese don't drink alone. You never lift your glass by yourself. It's always in response to a toast. And there are many, many toasts.

- A toast is always "bottoms up." You empty your glass, then tip it over to demonstrate that it's empty (relax a little ... the glasses vary in size).

- If someone toasts you, you will always, but never immediately, toast them in return.

- You always stand for a toast. The larger the meal, the more often you'll be standing up. Wear comfortable shoes.

- You always say the same word when you toast: Ganbei. It's pronounced gahn-bay, which means "good health."

- When toasting, always defer to senior people in order of their seniority.

- With the immense exception of fortified rice wine (Wu liang ye), and Chinese-produced wines, the Chinese only drink the best. For senior management, nothing but top shelf. Hundreds of dollars for a bottle of wine is not uncommon – and the Chinese can fully deduct the cost as a business expense, unlike their American counterparts.

- If you are hosting a meal for senior Chinese business-people, you must provide unlimited access to massive quantities of alcohol. The more important you are, the more attention you must pay to what you're giving people to drink. The name on the label (and the high price tag) are more important than the taste.

- Like a banquet, the accompanying drinking is a ballet, featuring multiple toasts at multiple tables. Sometimes multiple people will toast you at the same time, so in return, you only have to go to their table once, and toast them as a group.

Still with us? We know this can be complicated at first (it certainly was for us). Here's more:

- You will most likely be toasted by everyone at the banquet, and in turn toast everyone else -- especially if you're the honored guest (and probably the only American in the room).

- If you don't like to drink or can't drink for any other reason, you can beg off by saying you're taking medicine. That's probably your only out. A banquet is not the place to come out as a recovering alcoholic.

- Even when drunk, subordinates are always deferential to superiors and observe boundaries.

- The Chinese can be very confrontational with each other during the business day with people at their own level, up to and including calling each other "liar," but at the end of the day they'll drop it and go out drinking at a banquet.

- The typical pattern is heavy drinking at evening banquets, but not a word about it the next day (at least not a word an American would hear or understand).

- As our catchy book title suggests, Chinese women are in a separate category when it comes to drinking. They're simply better at it. An important note: for Chinese business women, drinking is not a prelude to sexual advances. They're simply accommodating the macho drinking culture.

- We've seen women in "drinking challenges" (more on that later) with senior executives. It was clear that the women were holding their alcohol better than their male counterparts, and would have easily won the challenge. But, in every instance, because the women were lower in the company hierarchy that the challenging men, they found a way to opt out of the competition to allow the men to save face (more on that later too).

- You will be respected for your ability to drink (just as it's a really good idea to learn how to use chopsticks). It is important for others to see you as someone who can keep up, even though it will never be discussed the next day.

- All Chinese will be deferential to you as a guest if you're in China.

- We don't mean to imply that all Chinese are blazing a trail towards alcohol abuse and alcoholism. The drinking-infused banquets and challenges are just what we observed (and participated in). In the States, we have Chinese friends who won't touch alcohol. As one of them says, "It's wasted on me. I can't metabolize alcohol." Actually, the opposite is probably true: Asians metabolize liquor better than Americans do. It's because of the genetic coding for alcohol enzymes commonly found in Asians that is usually lacking among Westerners. We're not going to go into the science (because we're not scientists), but the bottom line is that many of the Chinese you'll drink with feel the buzz of alcohol less than you will. Much less.

CASE STUDY

Let's walk through the process with David, who has been to China several times over the past few years, and has gotten to be fairly comfortable with a group of colleagues (though he is not fluent or even conversant in Mandarin). David and his colleagues all work for the same Chinese company.

With each trip, David has learned more and more about the differences between how Americans and Chinese drink. In the States, it's common practice for groups of coworkers to go out to a bar after work, have a few drinks, then go their separate ways. In China, that doesn't happen – at least at the senior level. Colleagues don't go out to bars for drinks, but instead go out for business dinners where the drinking lasts for several hours, and gets more serious as the evening progresses. The company picks up the tab.

Remember Tom's experience with the food in the last chapter. Now it's time to go to dinner with David. You'll notice a lot of overlap.

Just like Tom's meal from hell, the dinner for David, who's the sole American colleague on this trip to China, is set in one of the private banquet rooms of a huge restaurant. In this case, though (because it facilitates the points we want to make about drinking) the room is set up with three tables, each seating 10.

Great Wall red wine arrives as soon as the food does. It's on the table, ready to pour, with the appetizer course. Remember, this wine is not being poured to sip and savor with food. It's being poured to guzzle when there's a toast. The glasses are relatively small, holding about four ounces.

The first toast is from the senior person at the table, the company president, to David as the guest of honor. There's no firm order of toasting, so there may be a bit of variance here, but typically the senior person toasts the guest first. David has been to meals like this before, and as his host stands to toast him, he stands to receive the toast, they both chant "Ganbei," empty their glasses, turn them over, and sit down.

Once the first toast has passed, the floodgates are open. Others can start toasting each other at any of the three tables. In each case, the participants swiftly rise for the toast, and then sit until the next one. David is wearing his orthotic shoes, because he knows he's in for a lot of jumping up and down.

There's no music in the room, but by the third course there have been a lot of toasts and the volume of chatter is going up. Remember, each of these toasts requires the participants to drink whatever is in their glass, and right now the glasses are not being poured to the rim. Soon they switch to high-alcohol content fortified rice wine. People are feeling good, and lots of smiles are evident through the room.

It's time for the drinking challenges to begin. We weren't kidding when we said Chinese business people drink like American college students. Compare the challenges to the pre-game festivities on any university football Saturday. It's perhaps a little classier in China, but they're essentially tailgating.

David is somewhat known and respected as being a good eater and sporting drinker. Let's call the challenger Mr. Zhu. He doesn't actually issue any sort of challenge in words. It's all in his actions. He offers David a toast, but then, as soon as the glasses are empty, Mr. Zhu does not sit down. He refills both glasses. Heads perk up at the other two tables, and there's a suspension of toasts at other tables for this challenge.

Here's another similarity to American tailgating: Wu liang ye is a lot like tequila, peppermint schnapps, and fortified wines. It's meant to be drunk quickly. Here's the difference: Wu liang ye is much worse. It smells a little like turpentine, and tastes like nasty medicine. This ain't sake. The only thing to be said for it is that it slides down fast. Also, it may bring some relief to note that toasts don't necessarily have to be done with full glasses, and in fact will only assuredly be full if there's a serious challenge going on. Which is what David is facing right now.

His Dad always said that David was never one to run away from a challenge. The pair knocks back the second glass, wish each other good health, turn their glasses upside down, and David motions for their glasses to be refilled. Smiles all around the room – this American knows how to play the game.

In case you're counting, Round Three means that each participant has consumed three glasses within a minute. There is little if any pause between toasts. David is feeling a warm glow.

Round Four: Mr. Zhu toasts to David's good health and camaraderie. Imagine downing two martinis in less than five minutes. That's about where David is right now. How long can this go on? Falling-down drunk is not uncommon at one of these banquets (and, keep in mind all that luscious food being consumed at the same time).

As Round Five commences, a twist. Remember how we said that Chinese women are the masters of this game? Mercifully, David's mentor at the company is a middle-aged Chinese woman. Let's call her Madam Huo. [Women in Chinese business of a certain age are given the honorific "Madam" title.] She steps forward, obviously concerned that David is not sufficiently experienced in this macho game, and she reduces the amount in his glass from four full ounces to about one ounce. Remember, you do have the option in these challenges, when you're doing the toasting, of deciding how much goes in the glass. There's no dishonor in toning it down so you don't end up vomiting in the corner.

Round Six, Mr. Zhu returns David's toast, but now with a fourth as much alcohol. We're probably up to about 18 ounces total.

Madam Huo knows that 18 ounces is more than enough. She intervenes again, this time to pull David away for a quick talk. Another challenge begins at another table, and she takes David to that table to observe rather than participate. His challenge is over (technically, he lost, and if you weren't watching the clock, it only took four minutes), but it doesn't matter as the room's attention has shifted to another challenge.

Two contests up, two contests down, and a good portion of the banquet's food has been consumed. Then, the company's president stands up, and offers a challenge to (who else), Madam Huo. Can you guess how this one will play out?

Of course, Madam Huo accepts the challenge. The president is her boss, though she's fairly senior herself. In this challenge, the glasses start with one-ounce portions (still, that's a small shot) and increases to full glasses within minutes.

David's challenge went six rounds. The contest between the president and Madam Huo will go at least 12.

By about Round Eight, the president is clearly in the bag. He's red faced, and getting more flushed with each shot. Madam Huo looks unfazed, and is not showing any signs of serious inebriation.

At Round Thirteen, Madam Huo (serious company player that she is) knows she needs to end this. But, she also knows that she should not win a contest against her business superior. He must be allowed to save face. So, she demurely stops the challenge, by simply smiling and saying she can't go on. The president is the winner, and acknowledges the cheers of the room as he slumps down into his chair.

David looks with admiration at his mentor, who is obviously the smartest person in the room.

ALCOHOL LESSONS

1. During a meal, never pick up your wine glass unless you're being toasted or offering a toast.
2. There will be continuous toasting throughout a meal. Remember that wine is not being served to enjoy with your food. It's there exclusively for toasting.
3. You always need to rise for a toast.
4. Make certain that you always return a toast at some point during the evening.
5. A toast doesn't have to be a full glass.
6. After a toast, always turn your glass upside down or tilt your glass towards your toaster to demonstrate it's empty.
7. Cocktails are not part of the Chinese tradition, but are gaining more acceptance ... especially single malt scotch and fine French cognacs (signs of prestige).
8. It's not considered bad form to get fall-down drunk. You'll hate yourself the next day, of course.
9. Tonight's drinking is not discussed tomorrow.
10. Never try to drink a Chinese woman under the table, unless you're her boss.

SIDEBAR:
Asians and Alcohol

As we noted in the preceding chapter, many of the Asians you'll drink with feel the buzz of alcohol less than you do. A lot less.

It's part of a package ... they often don't get drunk as quickly as Westerners, but many do get "Asian Flush Syndrome," in which an excess of alcohol causes an individual's face or body to flush or get blotchy (remember the company president from our case study, who got flushed?). Also, this syndrome has been associated with a greater risk of esophageal cancer.

So what does it mean for you? Just remember that if you get into a drinking challenge, you may have lost before you start. Making the toasts less than a full glass and getting it over quickly may be your best bets. Unless you like to fall down.

And, if you just go out for casual drinks with Asian colleagues, keep in mind that two or three or four for you might be one for them.

If you've already had experience in this area, especially in Asian countries other than China, we'd love to hear from you at our blog:

Never Try to Drink a Chinese Woman Under the Table
[Plus Other Fun and Practical Tips]
www.nevertrythis.net

We also compiled a quick starter list of the most popular drinks in the same countries we surveyed for our chapter on food. Take a look, and let us know if we've got it right (and, of course, if there are country-specific drinks that the adventurous business person simply must try, and if there are any drinking-related customs that Americans should observe).

JAPAN

- Beer is reportedly the most popular alcoholic drink in Japan.
- The leading breweries are Asahi, Kirin, Suntory and Sapporo. Suntory makes a world-class whiskey.
- Shochu is a traditional hard liquor made from distilled grains, and has become increasingly popular in New York via shochu-based cocktails.

PHILIPPINES

- San Miguel Beer.
- Gin.

SOUTH KOREA

- Soju (rice-based alcoholic beverage).
- Koreans pour and receive alcohol using two hands or one hand supporting the other.
- We've been told that it's considered courteous to wait until someone's glass is empty before pouring more alcohol. No topping off.

INDONESIA

- Not a big drinking country with its majority Muslim population.

THAILAND

- Rice whisky.
- Beer.

SEX

Do It, But Don't Discuss It

QUICK HELLO TO those prospective readers who picked us up off the bookstore shelf because of our snappy title, then immediately turned to this chapter because it's about sex. This book comes from a couple of guys who write about serious topics with a sense of humor. In this chapter, we're going to make the case that there's a revolution underway right now in China – a sexual revolution!

Now, go buy the book so you can get the whole story.

Okay, we're back for all of you—from the beginning readers to the slackers who just joined us.

As we make the case that there's a sexual revolution underway now that's at least as significant as Mao's cruel Cultural Revolution, we need to go back a few centuries. If you have any doubt that sexuality was a core focus of China's earlier dynasties, go review some of the art. Not the woodcuts and silk screens of delicate flowers and graceful dancers. The nasty stuff. You know what we mean, right? The explicit and arguably pornographic depictions of sex in line drawings. Opium dens teeming with illicit sex. The tales of concubines and eunuchs. Historically, the Chinese revered sex (at least privately) and celebrated its importance to their culture through art and in the entourages kept by the elites.

You'd never know it, of course, by looking at any of the visual depictions of last century's Cultural Revolution. Mao personally reveled in sex, and is reported to have had a continuous retinue of women pass through his bedroom. For the worker (peasant) class, sex was about procreation, and the production of more peasants. Mao viewed the mass of Chinese humanity as little more than ants – tools of his Communist worldview – and decreed that they be outfitted as such. The dress code: drab, sexless, green-grey uniforms.

Couples came together and stayed together to survive the government-initiated economic and cultural storms. Needless to say, there wasn't much energy left over. Whatever they had, the typical Chinese couple poured into their child, with a greater ferocity of purpose than parents in most other cultures. The population exploded, of course, leading to the adoption of the "One Child Policy" in 1979 (after Mao had left the scene).

The incessant doting on and promotion of the single child hasn't changed, but so much else has: China's new Cultural Revolution is a sexual revolution. In many ways, it's like the American Sexual Revolution that started around the '60s. Here's what we mean:

- For Americans of a certain age (say, over 45), it was extremely uncommon to have any friends with divorced parents as you were growing up. Then, the divorce rate ballooned, and now about half of all American marriages end in divorce. Same thing in China, at least in urban areas like Beijing. Divorce used to be rare, and certainly never discussed. For the past decade, the urban divorce rate has been rising into rates nearing 40 percent (it's still quite low in rural Chinese areas).

- The escalating middle-class divorce rate, we would argue, is a direct result of China's urban economic prosperity. When life is hard, you stick with what you've got and try to make the best of it. When times are better, options become evident. Why stay in a loveless marriage when you know you can survive on your own (even with children)? Why not try for a better and happier life?

- The drab, sexless attire of the Cultural Revolution has disappeared. All of the top European and American fashion designers have set up shop in China, and both genders have become avid shoppers – not to mention status-conscious brand buyers (more on that in our chapter on "Name Brand Status"). We've also noticed that for Chinese women working in America, provocative clothing is not unusual – and that it's often worn by divorced (and beautiful) 30-somethings with children. Trendy fashion has become a way for Asian women to set themselves apart when working in the West.

- Women within China ironically enjoy greater business advancement opportunities than their counterparts in the West. There's still a glass ceiling, but the glass is thinner and easier to crack. We think this is one of the few positive legacies of the Cultural Revolution: boys and girls alike were separated from their families, and endured equally grueling experiences at collective urban farms and re-education centers. When it finally ended and they were reunited with their families, there wasn't such a rigid distinction between men's and women's work – which carried over into the business realm for the generation that initiated China's explosive economic growth.

- But alas, some things don't change, no matter the culture: it's not uncommon to find married Chinese men working in America who have affairs with younger Chinese women at the office. This looks like a simple power-and-control dynamic to us. The Chinese remain very deferential to authority, both personally and in business settings. We think a lot of these affairs happen because Chinese men know they can hit on Chinese women of lower authority with little fear of repercussions. There is probably some status boost for Chinese men in having outside-of-marriage sexual conquests.

  And, sadly, the women often acquiesce because they don't think they have the option to say no.

- Within a Chinese-owned company in the West, you're likely to find instances of married Chinese men having Western (i.e., white) girlfriends. Can you say: "Trophy?"

- We haven't seen many instances of Western men having

affairs with Chinese women in Chinese-owned companies. Remember that expression, "Don't s**t where you eat?" It comes into play here. Chinese-owned companies are not known for privacy. Everyone knows everyone else's business, most of which is shared by the Chinese with each other, but not often with the Westerners. There wouldn't be a lot of cover available for an American man getting it on with a woman from the home country (we'll talk more later about the levels of hierarchy within a Chinese-owned company. For now, suffice it to say that the Americans and other Westerners don't come out on top. Pardon the pun).

- Beware of the interplay between office and sexual politics: we know of an instance where a senior American manager of a Chinese-owned business received an anonymous message from someone saying they were "very concerned about our company's reputation," because two company officers were carrying on an affair. Both were expats, married with children, one of them living in the states with his wife, the other with a husband and child back in China. The message said they were carrying on in public, exhibiting very bad behavior, and that of course this was interfering with their work. There are a few options for what was going on here, and all of them had at their root a desire to hurt the couple (if they even were a couple).

- For men: if you go to China on business, especially to Beijing, prepare to be terrified the first time your car pulls up to a hotel. The doors will fly open, and leaflets will be aggressively deposited by several promoters featuring pictures of beautiful and sexy Asian women (not wearing much clothing). Each leaflet will feature a phone number – call it, and a call girl will be delivered to your hotel door. This sort of rampant leafleting and sexual commerce happens with the full knowledge of (and probably payment to) the hotels. Welcome to the capital of China!

- There is an emerging gay culture in China, albeit one that looks a lot like America's from a few decades ago, featuring openly gay entertainment personalities and designers. There's some level of organization, especially at levels close to the elites. In many ways, it reminds us of the old tales about Ron and Nancy Reagan – lots of gay friends, but no one really talked about them being gay.

CASE STUDY

We want to illustrate how a cutting-edge sexual revolution scenario can play out in the context of a culture that maintains many of its historical cultural imperatives.

Simon is a 21-year old junior at New York University. His parents are well-connected in his hometown of Shanghai, and have nurtured and promoted Simon since the day he was born. He has taken classes in everything, and was well-prepared for his entrée into American business via study at a top U.S. university. Once his undergrad and graduate educations are complete, Simon's parents foresee a successful career for him in international finance, an equally accomplished wife from a similar family, and a beautiful grandchild. He is well aware that in exchange for their devotion to him, Simon's parents expect to be cared for by him as they age.

Simon's parents pay the full cost of his two-bedroom apartment in Greenwich Village, and use the extra bedroom themselves during their regular visits to New York. When in the States, they love taking Simon to expensive dinners and the newest musicals on Broadway.

When the folks are in town, Simon's American boyfriend Dave stays with friends a few blocks away from their apartment. They both hate the façade, but Dave buys Simon's reasoning that it's necessary. Simon hasn't told Dave about his parents' fantasy of a wife and child. [Actually, it could still happen.]

Though in the closet to his parents, Simon is relatively out at the Chinese-owned financial services firm where his parents arranged a summer internship. Since privacy is unheard of in a Chinese-owned business, Simon was probably smart to be open about his sexuality – and knew there was almost zero chance of it ever getting back to mom and dad.

Simon is a summer hit at the company. He's smart and personable and talented. He works well with others. He gets assignments completed ahead of deadline, and is always available and eager to pitch in as new things come up. He would be an asset to any business.

But then, about two months in, something happens. Simon disappears, and word starts to circulate that he unexpectedly resigned, and his resignation was accepted without question. "Move on" is the unspoken message everyone receives.

What happened? One of Simon's Chinese woman friends at the company is determined to find out. It isn't easy: Simon does not answer emails nor responds to messages, and she doesn't know his home address.

Then serendipity intervenes, and she bumps into Simon one evening on the street. She grabs his hand, literally pulls him into a bar, sits him down, and makes it abundantly clear that he's not moving until he spills.

Spill he does: over the course of several drinks, an increasingly relaxed and forthcoming Simon tells the story of the Chinese chief of his old division, a married man with a wife and child back in China.   He was reportedly going through a divorce.

Simon says that the chief started hitting on him shortly after his arrival. At first, it was just casual flirtation which Simon (having no interest) was able to divert.

But the chief was one of those guys trained to never take no for an answer. He kept escalating his advances, including the buying of several gifts which he would not take back and Simon started to keep in a locked desk drawer.

"Why didn't you report him, or fight back?" Simon's Chinese friend, sounding very American, wanted to know.

"Because I couldn't win, and the fight would threaten my professional life here and potentially devastate my parents," Simon said, sounding very much like the Chinese man he was born and raised to be.

Simon went back to school, and his lecherous boss was free to wait for his next victim.

55

SEX LESSONS

Here are just some of the things we want you to remember from the front lines of China's sexual revolution:

1. Like most things, China's current thinking and cultural practices are steeped in history: Sexuality was relatively open in earlier periods, shut like a steel trap door during the Cultural Revolution, and is quickly evolving today to a more Western approach.

2. China's sexual revolution is still very much informed by two cultural imperatives that were strengthened during the Cultural Revolution: "everything-for-the-child," and "utmost-respect-for-the-parents."

3. China's recent prosperity has been foundational to its sexual revolution: in a society that is no longer hand-to-mouth (at least for the urban elites), divorce is acceptable as people try to maximize their happiness and success.

4. Also as the result of economic prosperity, the Chinese are able to indulge in cutting-edge aesthetics and fashion – at least at the level of their Western counterparts, but probably more so because the Chinese are especially motivated by the status and cache of being cutting-edge. This results in provocative displays of distinctive apparel and styling, especially among young Chinese women doing business in Western countries. It's tamer back home.

5. Chinese men sometimes take advantage of the deference typically shown to superiors within a professional environment. They have affairs with Chinese women of a lower rank, who may feel they have no choice but to say yes.

6. The many Chinese students studying in the States and elsewhere are their parents' children. They may well take advantage of the liberal options presented to them by Western cultures, while at the same time honoring the traditions that were a very significant part of their upbringing. As any shrink will tell you, it's not an easy thing to keep one foot in two different worlds.

7. Chinese women enjoy greater career mobility than their counterparts in many Western economies.

8. Chinese men working in Chinese companies in the States or other Western countries will often consider an affair with a local woman (i.e., white) as something of a trophy relationship, and could enjoy the experience as a status-booster.

9. The line between sexual politics and office politics can easily blur.

10. If you're an American man, considering an affair with a Chinese counterpart, we urge caution. "Never try to drink an Asian woman under the table" is a concept that could easily be applied to this realm.

SIDEBAR:
Asians and Sex

Let's take a little trip to an Asian country outside of China, one known as the international capital of sex vacations (for men). Can you guess which country we're talking about?

Yup: Thailand. And, Bangkok in particular.

In the tourist and red-light districts of Bangkok, you'll see more sex businesses on each street than you're able to count. And, you'll notice hawkers outside beckoning you in for a look as to why theirs is the best, and worth your time (and money). It's probably not an overstatement to say that anything and everything is available 24/7.

The specialty in Bangkok is "The Soapy." It's pretty much as it sounds – a naked masseur or masseuse, lots and lots of suds, and a "Happy Ending." It's just one of many "services" available, and quite explicitly charged for. Actually, there's usually a basic fee, then a list of other amenities, each with a corresponding gratuity.

You'll also find plenty of bars and clubs with scantily-clad (if they're clad at all) pole dancers. They will sit on your lap, and hug and kiss you. If you buy them a beer, you are their "Sugar Daddy." Their ultimate goal is a private session in the back room.

We'd love to hear about your experiences and any anec-dotes you want to share about sex in Asia or in Western countries – especially as it relates to the experience of people doing business. If you want to keep your privacy by posting anonymously, we're fine with that. Please do pick a clever screen name (just because we appreciate being amused), and – our one serious note – understand that we'll delete anything that crosses the line into obscenity or furthers unfair and inaccurate cultural stereotypes:

> Never Try to Drink a Chinese Woman Under the Table
> [Plus Other Fun and Practical Tips]
> www.nevertrythis.net

Your Chinese Colleagues:

How They Think

Why They Keep to Themselves

How That's Changing

GENERATIONAL CHANGE:

The Aging Revolutionaries, the Questioning Middle, and the Start-Ups

THERE ARE THREE distinct generations of Chinese now doing business, and it's important that you know who they are. The major observable difference between them is of course their age, but it's necessary to look beyond that. Americans often catalog changes between generations in terms of how they looked (hairstyles, clothes) and what they did (music they danced to, etc.). The differences between Chinese generations were shaped by their fundamentally different childhoods.

China went through a massive social upheaval in the past 40 years, moving from the end of the oppressive Cultural

Revolution through President Nixon's "Ping Pong Diplomacy" and then a gradual opening to Western business (but not Western traditions of transparency and democracy). The three current business generations were internally stamped by what they experienced (and, especially for the oldest, what they endured).

We've named the three generations, and listed important characteristics of each:

The Aging Revolutionaries – Business leaders now in their 50's and 60's

- The first generation to come to power in "modern" China. They are its face, and at the pinnacle of power.

- These folks are not fashion plates. They wear drab clothes, have Mao-era hairstyles, and are unlikely to speak English (especially those outside Beijing and Shanghai).

- The Aging Revolutionaries are the children of those who lived under the closed system of 40 years ago. They were school kids during the Cultural Revolution.

- During the Cultural Revolution, education was suspended and schools were closed. Chinese society's focus shifted to the creation of an agrarian collective workers society. If children lived in an urban environment back then, they were literally ripped from their homes and sent to work in the fields.

- As the Cultural Revolution came to an end, teenagers

returned home and resumed their education.

- This one is critical: They also came home with very strong bonds to other kids they lived with during their countryside stays. Many of those relationships endure today, and significantly impact the way they do business. The closest Americans come to this are the alumni connections from our undergrad or graduate school experiences. But, what do you think would be stronger: bonds forged over tailgate parties and a few all-nighters, or bonds from the shared survival experience of spending 12 hours a day, seven days a week doing the backbreaking work of harvesting crops, with breaks for cultural reeducation, over the course of several years?

- Appearances can be deceiving. The Chinese will not easily display the ferocity of their indoctrination and what they went through. There's no question, though, as to where their loyalties lie. They suffered tremendously, arguably sacrificed their youth, but are also the first generation in modern China to get a taste of real wealth.

- Aging Revolutionaries had their own children later in life because their formative years were interrupted.

- Though their current significance is profound, senior business leaders are slowly aging out, because state-controlled businesses have a mandatory retirement age of 55 for women and 60 for most men.

The Questioning Middle – Mid-level managers in their 30's and 40's

- Couples in this middle group, if they're posted in the United States, typically have a single child attending an American school. These couples did not endure the Cultural Revolution's massive relocation, and their own Chinese educations were not interrupted.

- At least one person in these couples is a mid-level manager, steadily moving up the business hierarchy. As they move from their 30's into their 40's, they'll assume positions of real responsibility.

- We call this group the "Questioning" Middle because they did not go through the Cultural Revolution's indoctrination as the Aging Revolutionaries did. As a result, they can be conflicted about being able to accept their Chinese political and social education without questioning it – particularly if they've spent some time outside of China. Expats have a broader world view.

- We're trying to stay out of politics as much as we can in this book, but it's our repeated observation that the Questioning Middle is much more of a challenge for their government than the Aging Revolutionaries are, because they might question things. They grew up as China was going through its modernizations. They were exposed to the West, albeit in a very censored fashion. As a result, they have a more comprehensive worldview.

- When working outside of China for a Chinese company, a woman who becomes pregnant is required to return to China to give birth. Couples of this generation will usually have just one child.

- Their children quickly assimilate into American culture. Kids are easily Americanized, and you really start to see it with Questioning Middle's children. It's often very difficult for parents to get these kids to study and speak Mandarin. We've seen a number of instances where the parents will speak in Mandarin, but the child will only answer in English. Rebellion of a mild sort, but rebellion nonetheless.

- If they move back to China after a typical five-year business posting in the U.S., families may split up so that children can stay here and continue in American schools (which are generally perceived as superior to those in China). Oftentimes the husband will return to China or another foreign post, while the wife stays in the U.S. with their child.

- Since the educational systems are so different, it's typical for returning students to lose a year of education in China. A student who completes third grade in America will probably have to do it again in China – with an educational system built much more on rote learning than in U.S. schools.

The Start-Ups – Business people in their 20's, new to the game

- First, a note on China's "one child" policy. This regulation has been softening, but that's just been over the past few years. Now, if a husband and wife each come from single-child families, they are allowed to have two children. Start-Ups themselves are from single-child households (their parents are often Aging Revolutionaries). Even though they're now permitted two children, it often makes much more economic sense to maintain a single-child home.

- These young adults, now in their 20's, have been the sole or narrow focus of their parents' attention, and they are the beneficiaries of parents' willingness to sacrifice whatever is necessary to provide the Start-Ups with opportunities.

- The sacrifices of Chinese parents mean very high expectations for Start-Ups. It's no accident that many of the top slots in American schools are filled by driven Chinese students.

- Placement in top U.S. prep schools and universities confers status on the parents (see more on Name Brand Status in the following chapter).

- Their parents' extensive business contacts help place the Start-Ups in top summer internships and post-college entry-level training programs at top financial firms.

CASE STUDY

Let's put some faces on the three generations. They wouldn't realistically be from the same family, because the Chinese government would not allow three generations of one family to be in the United States at the same time. So, let's say they're all from the same city: Wuhan, in Hubei Province (the most populous city in central China). It's known as one of the Three Furnaces of China, because it gets so hot and humid there in the summer.

The Aging Revolutionaries are Mr. Chu and Madam Pang, a 50-something married couple (Chinese women typically do not take their mate's surname when they marry ... and remember that women in Pang's age range are usually called "Madam"). They grew up in Wuhan, and have known each other since their school was closed and they were sent to a workers colony for work and "study." Their adolescence was punctuated by field work in the mornings, re-education in the early afternoons, a return to the fields in the late afternoons, and evenings spent playing games, singing songs, and learning to march – all exercises designed to heighten their appreciation of the Chinese state, and increase their devotion to it. There was absolutely no outside influence – no foreign movies, television, newspapers, books, or ideas. They accepted their situation without question (dissent was simply unheard of).

After the Cultural Revolution ended, they returned to Wuhan for a few years of a more conventional education. They were proud to be invited to join the Party, and got married in their early '30s. Over the years, both worked their way through the business ranks – Mr. Chu at a state-controlled farm implements manufacturer, and Madam Pang a manager at the Hubei Provincial Museum.

In the Chinese version of the American Dream, these Aging Revolutionaries have a lovely home, which they've expanded and renovated a few times. Their household income has grown considerably over the years, allowing them to buy elegant clothing for their occasional nights out, a new BMW, and air travel to other parts of China during their vacations.

Unlike many pursuing the American Dream, however, the major asset of Mr. Chu and Madam Pang is not their house. It is unquestionably their 20-year-old daughter, who likes to be known by her chosen American name – Sophia.

Her parents never considered a home improvement or vacation for themselves until Sophia's every real or perceived need was met. Since an early age, she has taken private voice and dance lessons, had a private tutor in addition to her state-provided education, and most recently a barrage of assistance to help prepare her applications to American universities. Sophia is a very disciplined and determined young woman, speaks almost fluent English, and was accepted at Harvard (and there's no one in Wuhan who hasn't heard about it from her proud parents).

While Mr. Chu and Madam Pang are Aging Revolutionaries, with their adolescence marked by deprivation and struggle, Sophia lives at the opposite end of the spectrum. She has never gone hungry, never been near a farm, and never had to settle for the education provided by the Chinese state. She's going to college in America! To us, she's a Start-Up.

Let's fast forward a bit, because we all know that Sophia will be a star at Harvard. She knows how to study, how to maintain inner discipline, how to take tests, and how to supplement her growing academic resume with continued music lessons and growing responsibility at Harvard's many service clubs. She also has the benefit of a lovely personality, and makes friends easily. The part we're most interested in is what Sophia does after graduation.

Mr. Chu and Madam Pang have had three years to nurture their network of contacts doing business in the States. Dad knows, and has done favors for, many people working in the manufacturing, legal, and finance sectors in the Northeast. Mom, with her experience at a leading Chinese museum, has many contacts in the American arts establishment.

Will Sophia have a full dance card of interviews while at Harvard, not to mention a number of internships to choose from for her junior-year summer? You bet she will. She wants to make her early mark as a businesswoman in America, and she will be completely teed up by her parents – with the expectation that she excel in everything she touches. She will also be provided with a menu of Chinese-born businessmen for dating purposes.

Finally, let's take a quick look at a couple from the Questioning Middle. Remember that they really can't be from the same Chu/Pang family, because we've never seen that many people from one family in the U.S. at the same time.

Mr. Qian and Ms. Chen are in their 30's (which explains why Chen is called Ms. and not Madam). He works in financial services for a Chinese company. They're in the third year of what they expect to be a five-year stint in New York. Since both are the offspring of single-child households, they were allowed to have two children, though of course Ms. Chen traveled back to China to spend the latter part of her pregnancies with her family there. The infants remained with their grandparents in China for their first two years, and are now enrolled in an American public elementary school.

Mr. Qian and Ms. Chen have given their children the very American names of Brett and Calista for use at their school and with their nanny. Both parents work very long days, and are sometimes concerned when the children call the nanny "Mom" by mistake – a very American problem, don't you think?

Both Mr. Qian and Ms. Chen are mindful that he'll need to make a move back to China, or accept another foreign posting, in two years when his proscribed American business lifespan comes to an end. They have already decided that Ms. Chen will stay behind with the children, allowing them to maximize their educational opportunities and the social and business network in New York City. Mr. Qian, for the good of the family he sincerely loves, will accept a posting wherever the company needs him. He hopes to at least stay in the Western Hemisphere, and is hoping for Canada or Central America.

They do not share their plans with any of their friends or colleagues – you'll see the significance of that in our Passport Paradox chapter.

GENERATIONAL CHANGE LESSONS

Okay, that was a quick dash through what we've observed about the three generations of Chinese doing business today. Here's a review of the lessons we want you to learn:

1. There are distinct groups of people with different worldviews, reflecting their experience, based on their age.

2. Members of the most senior Chinese generation now doing business at the senior level really suffered in their lives, accepted their position, didn't get embittered, they forged very powerful alliances that cross over industry boundaries.

3. Americans' expectations in business settings should be informed by the age-associated cultural influences on their Chinese counterparts.

4. Influences of educational access, also age-related, are very important.

5. There are significant challenges for the Chinese government to maintain control over the younger generations as Western influences become more pronounced.

6. It's common practice for the Internet to be censored in

China, but that doesn't prevent the flow of information to further inform the younger generations.

7. Parents' desire to provide opportunities to their child, or children, crosses generations and is a powerful influence. Both parents will typically work, sometimes in different cities, and grandparents often raise the children.

8. Status is an important motivator, especially noteworthy in the admissions race for prestigious schools in America.

9. Parents provide significant opportunity, but really do fulfill the "Tiger Mom" stereotype of keeping the expectations bar very high.

10. Teenage rebellion is not unknown by Chinese 30 - 40-somethings, whose efforts to teach Mandarin to their children are often openly resisted.

SIDEBAR:
Generations of Asians in Business

China may be the largest Asian country to undergo a generational upheaval in the past 50 years, but it's not the only one. China had its Cultural Revolution, which pulled children from their homes and cemented their ties to the government. Even as these revolutionaries age out, they still largely run the show. And, as we've shown, they have a sometimes uneasy relationship with the generations following them.

Two other Asian countries pop to mind that may have a lot in common with the Chinese experience.

VIETNAM

Though the American involvement was most evident during the '60s and '70s, Vietnam was basically at war for 20 years, from 1955-1975. Some demographers say the two decades of war basically wiped out an entire generation (and the birthrate certainly took a big dip).

What does that mean for business? Well, it's of no small consequence that about two-thirds of the population is now under age 39. Post-war Vietnam is a nation of the old and young, with not much of a middle-aged cohort. Remember that in China today's 50- and 60-somethings were subjected to a Cultural Revolution, but they weren't decimated. The Chinese returned to manage the economy and reap its economic rewards.

The World Bank and other sources say that Vietnam's economy has robust prospects for growth, perhaps outstripping the economies of Northern Europe within the next 10 years. So it's obviously a place of economic opportunity, and is already a major exporter of some agricultural products.

But if you want to do business with the Vietnamese, where do you go and who do you ask? We've heard (we stress "heard," we hope you'll fill in our blanks) that what used to be known as the "Harmonious Vietnamese Family," with several generations living under one roof, is dramatically changing.

CAMBODIA

The Vietnam War ended in 1975, at about the same time as the Khmer Rouge under Pol Pot assumed control in Cambodia. The country's agony was marked by the entire population being sent on forced marches to rural work projects. Western culture was completely rejected, and anyone perceived as being from the professional or educated class was targeted. As many as one-fourth of the population of eight million died from execution, exhaustion, overwork, starvation and disease.

Abuse was certainly common during China's Cultural Revolution, but we don't think it was as brutally systemic as what we've heard about from Cambodia. [It is interesting to note that China is now the largest foreign investor in Cambodia's economy – but of course China is a major investor in many other countries throughout Asia.]

Vietnam and Cambodia are just two examples we

picked of other countries that probably have at least as much generational disturbance as China had – with direct implications for those who are trying to do business now in those countries. Neither country has a fraction of the owned businesses in America that China has, so we're assuming that the most relevant question for businesspeople is now to navigate the situation there, versus working for a Vietnamese- or Cambodia-owned business here in the States.

But, what about the rest of Asia? Are there distinct generations now doing business, or do they simply tend to be people of different ages – perhaps with the older ones more conservative than the young, and less willing to take risk?

We admit that we really need help with this one. What do you think? Who do you know? Can you make generalized statements about the current generations of business people in particular Asian countries? Please let us know on our blog:

Never Try to Drink a Chinese Woman Under the Table
[Plus Other Fun and Practical Tips]
www.nevertrythis.net

NAME BRAND STATUS:

Let's Go Shopping!

WHEN YOU OPEN the newspaper or go online and read a story about China, do you think the Chinese are positioning themselves as a First World country, or do you think they're from what's essentially the Third World, albeit with industrial might and a bottomless well of inexpensive labor? If you think the latter, it's time to update your worldview. You've obviously never gone shopping with the Chinese.

Here's what you need to know:

- The middle class in China is huge. There are lots of potential shoppers. All three of the Chinese generations we've previously described are into it.

- The middle class is China's new wealthy class – there are lots of estimates out there, but a commonly used statistic is the 300 million people with college degrees (more than the entire U.S. population).

- In major Chinese cities, you'll have a hard time not tripping over the high-end shopping malls. They are everywhere. All the top international luxury firms have a huge presence in China -- Hermes, Tiffany, Louis Vuitton, Prada, Coach – along with the current flavor of the month among the fashionistas.

- When the Chinese travel abroad, they have two primary objectives: to go shopping, and to get their pictures taken next to famous attractions. In our experience, they don't feel an obligation to go inside the world's great museums. They just want a picture to document that they were in front of the National Gallery of Art.

- When traveling for business, it is very much the exception for the Chinese to travel alone. They're always with a delegation of from 6 to 50 (see more on this in our chapter on Going Solo versus Group Think).

- Any itinerary for business delegations always includes a significant amount of time for shopping (at least a full day on a five-day trip).

- When a group of traveling Chinese businesspeople go on a shopping excursion to a luxury outlet mall, they'll typically send along an extra van to carry their purchases (the luggage space under the bus seats wouldn't have the necessary capacity).

- Americans, including those working in the U.S. for Chinese companies, are not likely to get involved in the shopping excursions of visitors from China. If they are, it would be on very short notice (because the delegation doesn't have enough locals available to drive them and their purchases to and from the mall – see the upcoming Case Study).

- The Chinese usually stick to name-brand designers. They are logo buyers. If a Chinese shopper looks at a high-end item (scarf, jewelry, jeans) and can't see a logo, it'll get left on the shelf.

- It is common to spend hundreds of dollars for gifts for important people. In the United States, you might give a colleague a business card holder. That would be considered a bad joke in China (we love our humor ... just make sure your jokes are funny).

- Electronics have to be the latest and greatest. We remember one instance where a New York-based group of Chinese expats going to China bought 10 unlocked iPhones to take on a marketing trip. Apple announced a new version midweek, so on Friday they scoured the city for 10 new ones, found them, and discarded the "old" ones. They could not be returned for a refund.

- The same rules apply to alcohol purchases. The Chinese have become major purchasers of high-end French wines, single-malt Scotch, cognac, etc.

- Chinese designers are emerging as a new international force; keep an eye out for them.

- Members of Chinese delegations visiting the U.S. get a per diem allowance. Since all meals and lodging are already covered by their hosts, they are free to use their per diems to shop (though this is not discussed explicitly, everyone does it).

- When Chinese delegations visit New York, their "shopping" extends to Broadway shows, even though most members of the delegation speak little English. They simply have to see the season's most popular musical.

- High-end status shopping includes education. Though the rules have softened, China is still largely a one-child-per family country. Parents focus all their attention on their child's overseas education. There is intense parent-fueled and –funded competition to get into the top American prep schools and universities. This is of course a godsend for American prep school and university presidents and business school deans, because the Chinese pay in cash up front. They don't expect scholarships or financial aid. They also make hefty contributions to the schools in advance of filing applications (especially at the prep school level).

- Even a blizzard won't stop Chinese shoppers, which serves as a great transition to our Case Study...

CASE STUDY

As we said, as an American you're unlikely to get drafted to participate in a shopping expedition for a visiting Chinese delegation. But there's one way we've seen it happen: the local office is short on available drivers, and there's a blizzard prediction. Not even the experienced Chinese drivers know how to handle snow.

Sam, a five-year American veteran of a Chinese company's New York City office, gets a visit to his office at 4:48p.m. on a Friday afternoon, "asking" if he can help out with the visiting delegation's Saturday shopping trip. The weather forecast is for sleet, heavy winds, and a foot of snow. Sam's Midwestern common sense would say "cancel the trip," but he's been around this company long enough to know that's not an option. Also, he's in the running for a promotion, so saying "no" isn't an option. He doesn't have the necessary license to drive a bus, but can drive the large van being rented to haul the loot back from the shopping trip. He smiles, says, "I'd be honored to help," and calls his spouse to relay the news that their Saturday plans have to be rescheduled. He endures a long silence on the phone, and realizes this will not be a free ride on more than one level.

Very early Saturday morning, Sam steers his large but empty van behind a luxury motor coach as they make their way to Woodbury Commons, the premium outlet mall about an hour's drive outside New York. So far, the weather isn't too bad – just some sleet on the highway, but the wind is kicking up. Sam has spent the past few days in meetings with the 40 visiting Chinese, and knows how excited they are about their trip to an American shopping mall.

Woodbury Commons features several hundred stores, and it's worth noting that the store directory is printed in English, Spanish, and (you could guess, right?), Chinese. There's also a foreign currency exchange in the one of the food courts, as well as an international shipping office. There are also a few Chinese-themed fast food restaurants.

Sam's van follows the motor coach as the delegation is dropped off at the entrance near the Neiman Marcus and Saks Fifth Avenue outlets. The delegation's four guides (remember, the Chinese never travel alone) exchange cell phone numbers with the bus driver and Sam (who is now on call to swing by with the van whenever an individual shopper makes a significantly weighty purchase). During the exchange of numbers, Sam asks if it might be advisable to consider condensing the six hours devoted to this trip due to the weather forecast. The Chinese guides laugh, assuming Sam is making an American joke. Inclement weather does not stop a serious shopper, especially if she or he is Chinese (and the Chinese men are as excited about this expedition as the women).

Let's meet a few of the shoppers:

- Mr. Liu is shopping with his friend and colleague Mr. Ren. Both are in their late 30's, and this is their first trip to the United States. Both are married, and are carrying lists from their wives back in China with their assigned purchases. The lists include Hermes scarves, Coach bags, Prada belts, and Jimmy Choo shoes. [Yes, we know, ironically enough many of these products are actually manufactured back in China, but they're often made for export and are actually more expensive in China.] For themselves, Mr. Liu and Mr. Ren want Burberry trench coats, and plan to buy off-the-rack Ralph Lauren suits (which they think are superior to the custom-cut suits they're able to buy for a fraction of the price in China).

- Ms. Wang shops with Ms. Nie. They're also both in their early 30's and stylish dressers. Ms. Wang is married, and has a young child at home. Ms. Nie is single. Ms. Wang plans to buy clothing for her husband, her kid, and herself. Ms. Nie already has a full closet, and is targeting accessories (especially gold jewelry).

While Mr. Liu, Mr. Ren, Ms. Wang, and Ms. Nie consult the mall's map and maneuver around the acres of stores, poor Sam sits in the van. The weather has turned from sleet to snow, and sometimes the wind gusts make it appear as though the snow is falling sideways. He's seen this before. Back in the Midwest, it's the kind of weather that earns constant updates on television, marked with advisories to "only go outside if you absolutely have to!"

Sam fears not only for his guests, but for himself. The driver of a van in a weather-related highway crash would not be anyone's candidate for the office fast track. So, he pleads again to condense the shopping expedition before the weather gets worse. He even calls his boss. Sam is politely but firmly turned down.

NAME-BRAND STATUS LESSONS

Let's assume our story has a happy ending. The bus and Sam's van make it home in one piece. Sam is greeted warmly by his spouse, whose anger over the day's cancellation is replaced by sheer relief that Sam arrived back home at all.

What has Sam learned?

1. Shopping is more than recreation for the Chinese.

2. If you're giving a gift to a Chinese business colleague, make sure it's a name brand item.

3. Logos convey status.

4. Price conveys status. You can't go wrong if it's expensive.

5. If you can't buy it in China, that's the best possible gift (i.e., just-released American electronics).

6. Shopping time is scheduled, and an essential part of the itinerary, for any visiting business delegation.

7. You're not likely to get involved in a shopping outing as an American, but best to always be ready.

8. If you get sucked in, you're with the delegation as long as they need you.

9. If you're hosting Chinese businesspeople in the U.S., be sure to build in as many great shopping opportunities as you can.

10. Chinese men enjoy shopping as much as American women.

SIDEBAR:

Name Brand Status across Asia (and the World)

We think the pursuit of name-brand status, a universal across Chinese business, is also nearly universal among other Asian countries. [Of course, the same brands that make Asian shoppers glaze over have the same effect on Americans – the shoppers at New York's Woodbury Commons are certainly not exclusively Asian.]

So, rather than try to compare and contrast which bauble wows in Beijing but bombs in Bangkok, we thought it would be more fun to list the brands that are hits throughout the business world:

Shop Till You Drop (Or Your Wallet Does)

Top 25 International Brands to Impress Your Business Colleagues

(note: we're leaving out auto brands)

1. Apple
2. Louis Vuitton
3. Hermes
4. Tiffany
5. Prada
6. Coach
7. Jimmy Choo
8. Samsung

9. Mitsubishi
10. Sony
11. Hitachi
12. Disney
13. Nokia
14. Nike
15. Gucci
16. Cartier
17. Ralph Lauren
18. Burberry
19. Moet & Chandon
20. Tom Ford
21. Marc Jacobs
22. Versace
23. Saks Fifth Avenue
24. Harry Winston
25. Chanel

Well, what do you think? Have we got them all? Are there any items on this list that an American might love, but an Asian from a particular country might hate? Please let us know on our blog:

Never Try to Drink a Chinese Woman Under the Table [Plus Other Fun and Practical Tips]
www.nevertrythis.net

NEVER TRY TO DRINK A CHINESE WOMAN UNDER THE TABLE

LOSS OF FACE:
Where Did It Go?

I **N THIS CHAPTER WE'RE** going to talk about the biggest transgression – or sin – you can commit when doing business with the Chinese. You can get away with telling bad jokes (our specialty), being an idiot, lying, and maybe even stealing, but you will not get away with insulting someone publicly. In the Asian mindset, a public humiliation, or "loss of face," is the worst possible thing that can happen.

Here are the points we'll highlight in this chapter:

- Loss of face includes shame but has other connotations – none of them good.

- We believe the absolute aversion to loss of face has become so reinforced over the years that it is now an essential part of Asian DNA.

- Loss of face is important not only at the individual level, but rises from there to the very top – the way the country sees itself. Yes, China is a totalitarian state. Still, we think the fact that you never see anyone trashing China internally – let alone burning the flag as happens in the West – is significantly a cultural phenomenon.

- We talk elsewhere in this book about the active rumor mills at Chinese-owned companies. You may sense a contradiction. Isn't starting a rumor motivated by the desire to see someone lose face? Well, this gets into a bit of nuance, but in the world of Chinese business there seems to be a certain ability to distinguish between rumor and fact.

- In another chapter, titled "Who's to Blame?" we discuss the phenomenon of always finding someone to target for responsibility when something goes wrong, and that target is as far down the power chain as possible. Again, here's a bit of nuance: yes, of course the person getting blamed will lose face. But, it doesn't matter to those engineering the fall. To be blunt, to the extent they think about it all, they think they're squashing an insect. High-level decision makers usually don't worry about the fates of those on the low rungs. [Isn't that the way it works in the West as well?]

- The Chinese (and Asian) drive to succeed academically is tied in part to this aversion to loss of face. A student's success in school reflects well on the parents. Remember, most Chinese couples have only one child, and the tyke becomes the sole focus of their personal dreams. They can brag about a successful child. We feel sorry for those kids who don't measure up in their parents' eyes. Talk about a guilt trip!

- Don't equate loss of face with an aversion to speaking

out. The Chinese are extremely forthright. They don't observe many of the boundaries Westerners do, especially when it comes to what we'd think of as personal matters. Example: if you're in a private meeting with a Chinese colleague, and you happen to have put on a few pounds, you're likely to be told, "Hey, you're getting fat." This would never happen in public, because that would subject the individual to loss of face. In private, it's a different story.

- More on the crucial distinction between public and private, and the different boundaries you'll discover when interacting with the Chinese: if a colleague really messes up, he or she might be told that – quite directly – in a private meeting. But, if the same thing were to happen in a meeting with others present, then you'd have an intolerable loss of face situation. Whoever's doing the talking would create one or more enemies. Loss of face requires there to be a number of people in the room.

- Though loss of face is usually avoided, it may be the planned end result of a targeted campaign against an individual. In such a case, the actions leading to loss of face are very judiciously meted out. An astute observer can usually see it coming. An astute target may understand that such behavior is probably a signal that it's time to expeditiously seek a new job.

- You'll probably never see a brainstorming session – so typical in Western businesses – at a Chinese-owned company. Though the Chinese act by consensus whenever possible, brainstorms tend to highlight the individual over the group, and are therefore shunned. But aversion to loss of face is another motivator, because brainstorms are supposed to air any kind of an idea – even a bad one. In Chinese business, the bad idea would stick to the individual like glue.

CASE STUDY

Sharon never thought she'd go to work for a Chinese-owned company. She'd had a successful career in consumer product marketing, living on both coasts before settling in Chicago.

Sharon was one of those rare individuals who was liked as much as a person as she was respected as a competent manager of product launches. She was very forthright, and didn't make people wonder what she was thinking. At the same time, she tempered her professional honesty with a genuine interest in the people she worked with (a difficult thing to fake).

TripleSonic Products is a Chinese-owned holding company, which was formed to bring many household manufactured items under the same roof, and achieved amazing financial results for its owners in Shanghai.

Sharon was contacted by a recruiter she knew and trusted, who wanted to forward her as a candidate for a senior management position at TripleSonic.

'Not for me, but thanks," Sharon said.

"Why not?" asked the recruiter.

"Because I need to work in a transparent environment where it's okay to speak my mind," Sharon replied. "I've heard that's not how Chinese companies operate."

"This one is different," said the recruiter. "They know you by reputation, and are familiar with the results you delivered."

Sharon was curious, and went to meet executives at TripleSonic. She was more than pleasantly surprised. The mostly Chinese management staff was gracious, intelligent, and working on very big projects. They indicated a willingness to adequately fund a product launch, which Sharon knew was almost always a struggle. They said they were very open to new ideas, and expected to hear a lot of them from a new colleague. A lack of transparency may be the hallmark of other Chinese-owned companies, they said, but not at TripleSonic.

Meantime, life happened. Sharon's favorite boss was taken out in a management shake-up. She could no longer count on a base of support within her company. And the recruiter called with an increase in the salary offer.

Sharon made the switch, and enjoyed a wonderful initial six months at TripleSonic. She told her friends she was glad that things worked out the way they did. As she always stressed to her product teams, it takes time to really get the full measure of people.

At TripleSonic, it took about seven months.

Sharon was one of several senior managers involved in a new systems implementation. To say it was a disaster would be an understatement. The vendor – a major American player in the systems market – fell down at every opportunity. They sent kids to do the work of adults, while managers within TripleSonic missed several opportunities to prevent major problems.

It got really bad, really quick. Deadlines became the subject of internal jokes. One bad thing just kept building upon another, and managers tried to distance themselves as much as they could. Sharon was more than willing to take on responsibility, but found that her Chinese (and some Western) colleagues were going AWOL at critical junctures. And, the bad behavior was blatant. TripleSonic managers started skipping vendor meetings so as to avoid association with the failing project.

It all came to a head in a management meeting with several representatives of the outside systems vendor. A special guest from the home office in Shanghai also attended. The meeting started out innocuously enough, with a dry recitation of the project's timeline and a categorization of the many, many problems that had been happening.

Sharon sat in the room with an exasperated look on her face. What was the point of this recap? Everyone knew the problems! No one was willing to take any responsibility for them, let alone suggest a grand fix.

Sharon decided she had a choice: she could either say something, or her head would explode.

"Let's face it," she said with the trademark bluntness that would at least count in a Western firm for blowing off steam. "This is a complete and total mess, and I'm ashamed for all of us that we've allowed it to happen."

Remember – and this is critical – Sharon was not speaking to her colleagues in a private session. She was talking in an open forum with the outside vendor and with a visitor from the home office.

What happened? Silence. Complete silence.

Eventually, the meeting returned to the dry recitation

of the multiple problems and a nodded agreement at some temporary Band-Aids.

The only thing anyone would remember about the meeting was that Sharon had managed to cause loss of face for each and every one of her management colleagues, in the presence of outsiders and a home office executive! She became an object of derision, and someone to be avoided. The others began to privately speculate as to how long it would take for upper management to get rid of her.

LOSS OF FACE LESSONS

You can't help but feel bad for someone like Sharon. She knew what she was getting into at a Chinese-owned company, but made the common mistake of actually believing the assurances she received during the job courting process. What really did her in, though, was letting her building anger and frustration blow up into a situation where she could personally be held responsible for loss of face – not just for one other person, but for all her colleagues.

Some lessons to keep in mind:

1. "Loss of face" means causing someone to suffer humiliation in public.

2. Loss of face is among the worst transgressions that can happen in the Chinese culture.

3. An individual can experience loss of face, but in China it starts there and just goes up. No one in China wants to hear criticism of China. True, it's a totalitarian state, but loss of face is a cultural disaster at all levels.

4. Avoiding loss of face is a major motivator behind China's devotion to academic success. When you're an only child, you are strongly motivated to make your parents proud of you – and in China, most children are only children.

5. The Chinese want to avoid loss of face in public, but that doesn't mean they hold back in private. If you suck at your job, you will very likely hear about it.

6. If you do witness loss of face in public, it is probably part of a larger campaign to discredit a person. The Chinese think these things through.

7. The Chinese can be as blunt in person as they are gracious in public. What might be considered too personal to comment upon in western cultures – like someone's weight – will be fair game in private conversation with a Chinese person.

8. Chinese persons in upper echelons don't worry about loss of face for those at much lower levels in the hierarchy. Part of the function of people at lower levels is to take blame as needed.

9. One of the reasons brainstorming sessions don't happen at Chinese-owned businesses is that someone who presents a goofy idea will lose face.

10. Culture – developed over decades if not centuries – always trumps modern business practice and trends. "Transparency" is often touted as a goal among western businesses. With the Chinese ... well, they might talk it. The walk is a different matter.

SIDEBAR:

Asia Ain't the Place to Lose Your Face

We're fascinated by the way Asians seem to revere public perception of their cultures and leadership, and of course we think a lot of it has to do with the cultural aversion to loss of face.

A few noteworthy examples:

- In Thailand, it's against the law to publicly criticize the king. Performances of Rodgers & Hammerstein's "The King and I" are still forbidden.

- In Japan, disgraced business persons sometimes go beyond a public apology and resignation. They commit suicide.

- Our friends at the U.S. State Department say that although they pay attention to the protocol of all foreign powers, they are especially keen on the topic when dealing with Asia. They're always working to make sure that Asian countries are treated with the respect they feel entitled to – especially critical when setting up state visits, where who is in the room is at least as important as what is being said.

We know there's much more out there, and we'd love to hear what you know and have experienced first-hand. Please share on our blog:

Never Try to Drink a Chinese Woman Under the Table
[Plus Other Fun and Practical Tips]
www.nevertrythis.net

BIG NOSE:
More than How You Look

DO YOU LIKE YOUR NOSE?

Take a quick look in the mirror: is your nose too long, too wide, or just right? If you've had a nose job, are you satisfied with the results?

Okay, go back to your reading chair. No more need for a mirror, because how you actually look doesn't really matter to the Chinese. If you're a Westerner, you have a big nose.

More specifically, you are a "Big Nose."

Here are the points we'd like to highlight:

- Big Nose" is the Chinese popular term for Westerners in general.

- From the Chinese perspective, Westerners really do have big noses compared to Asians.

- Reality check: many Westerners do have longer noses. But, many Asians actually have wider noses and facial structures in general. This is just one of those cultural artifacts that are partly based in observable reality, and partly just an overrepresentation. It's been around a long time.

- There's also a fairly widespread perception among the Chinese that Big Noses – Westerners – can't really learn the Chinese language. There's a sense that Mandarin and Cantonese are so complicated and intricate that you really need to grow up in the culture to "get it." Yes, it's difficult – but not if you start at an early age.

- It's been said that, "beauty in China is a big Western nose." This is probably less so now than a few years ago, but some Chinese people have nose jobs to attain a more Western look. Similarly, skin whitening creams sell well in Chinese cities (and throughout Asia). It's hardly surprising: just look at the international appeal of Hollywood movies and other Western cultural influences. You don't see many Asian faces in blockbuster action flicks.

- The Chinese can be very superstitious, and often believe in "lucky" and "unlucky" faces. The nose is a central axis of the face, a "yin" stop in the balance between yin and yang. A large nose indicates wealth and prosperity.

- You might be getting the impression that Big Nose is a pejorative term. It's really not. It's more of a descriptor, and since it's associated with wealth, it can be a very good thing.

- In the world of business, a Big Nose is the Western face of a Chinese-owned enterprise. It's understood that Big Noses help to appease Western government regulators, and also indicate the worldliness and international reach of the business. Most large Chinese businesses in the West have Big Noses as the local face of the business.

- As detailed elsewhere in this book, Chinese expats are most often forced to live in a very insular community. Their employers essentially decide how much freedom they will have. When they arrive in the West, notably in the United States, they're not only told what they will do but also where they will live. The Big Nose separator is consistent with that: it's us versus them.

- We think a lot of the Big Nose phenomenon is attributable to basic human nature. Humans seek out their own kind. It provides a comfort level in a world with many uncontrollable aspects.

- Speaking of control, Big Noses don't have much of it. They are the Western face of a Chinese business, and probably have lofty titles, but they aren't making the big decisions. They're not high enough on the hierarchy scale, which we explicitly address in another chapter.

- Especially in some industries, Big Noses add a real level of comfort for Western government entities that regulate Chinese-owned business (particularly in sensitive areas like financial services). Again, it's just a case of Westerners being more comfortable with other Westerners, just as the Chinese are most comfortable with other Chinese.

- In a PR sense, Big Noses add real value. Within the local country, culture and economy, they add credibility and believability with important constituencies. And, of course, this is a common aspect not only of Chinese enterprises but businesses in general: when operating in a foreign country, they very often employ local talent.

- Not only do Big Noses act as the ambassadors in Western countries, we know of cases where they've been able to secure local secrets in competitive arenas, which allow Chinese-owned companies to effectively copy the industry leader.

- Another dynamic driving the prevalent use of Big Noses by Chinese business is the Chinese obsession with portraying themselves as new and modern. Even if the political tides are turning to more repression and human rights abuses at home, an all-inclusive spirit pervades abroad. Take a look at the websites of major Chinese companies. They look very international – lots of nationalities represented beyond their home base.

- Here's an example of the importance the Chinese place on a positive image among foreigners: at airports within China, it is common to give preferential landing and takeoff consideration to foreign carriers. If there's bad weather in Beijing, a United flight will get to land before one of the Chinese airlines. China wants you to know how modern and efficient it is!

- Another example: Rich was chosen to be an Olympic torch bearer in Tibet, with a full Chinese motorcade, because he wasn't Chinese.

- Forgive us, one more example: in advance of the Beijing Olympics, taxi drivers were taught English. The typically horrible Beijing traffic jams were alleviated by restrictions limiting native drivers to reduced days when they were allowed on the street. The streets were busy enough, so as to indicate prosperity, but not so busy as to suggest disorganization.

- If you are the Big Nose for a Chinese company, don't be deceived: you're not a player. You are a hired hand for a specific purpose. You won't be in the room when real decisions are made. If you are asked for input, there's a reason you are being asked.

- Best advice to prospective Big Noses: go in with your eyes open, and have your own plan. Know why you want this job, and what it can do for you. The most you'll be able to get up front on paper is probably salary and benefits. Try to initiate a discussion that will lead to a meaningful discussion. Once inside the door, set realistic goals, and maintain hyper-vigilance.

CASE STUDY

You know that admonition that all parents deliver to their children: "just be yourself!"

Let's see how well that works out for a Big Nose executive at a Chinese-owned business over the course of his career.

John has been in consumer electronics for 15 years, and has worked for a number of multinational firms. He's very well-regarded in the field, and has managed a few large product introductions.

Everyone in the business has heard about Spark Electronics, which has had a number of successes with innovative products that were a half step ahead of the competition and a price point below. Spark also does a considerable chunk of work for the U.S. General Services Administration, supplying inexpensive telephone system replacement parts for government offices.

But Spark, a Chinese-owned company headquartered in Shanghai with a considerable U.S. presence via its New York office, got into serious trouble. Several executives were rushed back to China in the wake of a money laundering scandal. Now, the American government regulators who had pronounced Spark a fit company to do business with just a few months ago have egg on their faces.

Spark engages a recruiter to find new local talent to help reposition itself. The recruiter goes right to John, and says he'd be an automatic finalist if he was interested. And there would be good money. No, there would be great money.

John is bored in his current job, and takes the bait. To say that Spark rolls out the red carpet is an understatement. John is made to feel wanted, needed and respected the instant he walks in the door. The general manager, Mr. Luck, is brand new in the job. He tells John – in almost perfect English – that he knows the electronics business, but does not know the ins and outs of American culture. Won't he please join Spark Electronics, and help guide the firm forward?

After feeling like he'd hit the ceiling at his last job, such flattering words seemed like a great gift to John, and Sparks' financial and benefits offer was competitive. He accepted.

John had a very clear path under Mr. Luck at Spark. He was able to smooth the ruffled feathers with the regulators, and offer assurances that Spark was a new company.

John really was a great fit in his new role. He'd never heard the descriptor "Big Nose," but certainly did feel as though he was the firm's American ambassador. He sat in on management meetings (though he couldn't understand anything of the Chinese being spoken). Everyone always smiled at him, and translations of the "important" parts were always provided to him.

John also got to travel the world on behalf of Spark. He was not only wined and dined in Shanghai, but was with the advance troops for every new Spark endeavor in the Western world. He even was chosen as one of the company's representatives when China's president traveled to the United States on a goodwill tour.

John spent several happy years at Spark, and was looking forward to a continuation when Mr. Luck announced he would be heading back to his family in China, to be succeeded by Mr. Su.

The early days with Mr. Su were even better than those with Mr. Luck. Mr. Su, again in almost perfect English, spoke passionately about his desire for a transparent and transformative workplace. John told his wife that Mr. Su had an open-door policy, and that his ideas were received with the greatest of interest.

But, alas, our story takes a twist. The air began to seep out of John's balloon. He started to notice that many of Mr. Su's words weren't matching Mr. Su's actions. Though a fervent advocate of workplace democracy, he began issuing dictatorial edicts. In the management meetings, John's meticulously prepared ideas were acknowledged, then ignored, then not even acknowledged.

John kept up appearances, because that was what he was being paid to do, but felt as though the wind was really going out of his sails the further that Spark got from its historic troubles. All those awful days of the money laundering scandal became a distant memory. And, disturbingly, all the senior Americans at Spark (the other Big Noses) were being removed from any real role in decision-making – before being physically removed from the office via buyouts!

John spent weekends with his wife, agonizing over what went wrong. He finally came to the obvious and inescapable conclusion: he was listened to only as long as he was really needed, and was never really a part of the decision-making team. He was still the same well-qualified individual who was so earnestly recruited by Spark Electronics. He didn't change, but he slowly came to understand what he had gotten himself into.

He had been hired as a Big Nose, though he didn't even know what that was. He did well with the first general manager, and quickly fell out of favor with the second. He was simply less valuable under the second regime. John befriended an executive in Human Resources, and was eventually able to negotiate a discreet buyout for himself.

BIG NOSE LESSONS

Let's note right away that what happened to John could happen to anyone, anywhere. What works under one regime may not work under another. Your perceived value to the company can always change. And, let's admit that we're human – even in a situation turning from good to bad, we'll try to find a silver lining, and hang onto it as long as we can. It's sometimes hard to perceive a shifting landscape when you're in the middle of it.

Here are the lessons to keep in mind:

1. The Chinese are just like everyone else: they align themselves to those with whom they share culture, language and history. They usually maintain a distance between themselves and others. They trust their own.

2. "Big Nose" is the moniker the Chinese often apply to Westerners. It's sort of reality-based, in that many Asians have shorter noses than Westerners (but theirs are often wider too, so go figure).

3. The function of a Big Nose is to provide a Western / international face at Chinese-owned businesses.

4. At the executive level, Big Noses often have lofty titles and large paychecks. But, they shouldn't kid themselves that they have real power. They're not in the room when decisions are made.

5. Big Noses are consistent with the Chinese obsession

with projecting themselves as modern and efficient and international.

6. Big Noses are also consistent with the tendency of the Chinese to keep to themselves in foreign postings. They live together, work together, and socialize together. As a Westerner, you're somewhat suspect.

7. Big Noses are especially useful for Chinese companies in dealing with American regulators, and especially after some sort of crisis when there's a huge need for new and trusting relationships.

8. Remember what happened to John with his first general manager: his services were needed in an obvious and critical way, and his value in helping to resurrect his employer's image was well-rewarded.

9. Also remember what happened to John after regime change: the memory of earlier crises faded, his services were not as essential, and his feedback was no longer encouraged.

10. Kenny Rogers probably wasn't thinking about the plight of Big Noses in Chinese-owned business, but his song lyric fits: you have to know when to hold them, and know when to fold them.

SIDEBAR:

Whose Nose?

As we've said, Big Noses present the Western or international face of Chinese-owned businesses in the West. They don't have any real power, though their titles and paychecks may indicate otherwise.

We'd love to hear from readers who can talk about the customs of other Asian cultures in this arena: do they also recruit locals and endow them with titles, pay, and no power? Are they similarly used to smooth the path for business with local governments and regulators?

We're fascinated by what we've heard about Japanese-owned businesses and their practice of dual management. There are two people in the Western office with similar or identical titles. One is a local, who does all the work and makes sure nothing bad happens. The other is a Japanese expat who does less but has a superior position in the decision-making apparatus.

So what do you think, what have you experienced, and what do you know?

And, yes, we'll take a few Big Nose jokes ... as long as they're really funny. Get in touch on our blog:

Never Try to Drink a Chinese Woman Under the Table
[Plus Other Fun and Practical Tips]
www.nevertrythis.net

LEARNING THE LANGUAGE:

You Have a Choice (or Two)

Remember your initial exposure to a foreign language? Probably back in high school, right? Depending on where you grew up, if your native language is English, you likely were required to take a year or two of German or Spanish or French. Beyond that, it was up to you. To learn Chinese, you would have to make a special effort, and be enrolled at a special school or had parents who forced supplementary or weekend lessons.

It's a very different situation for your potential Chinese colleagues, particularly since the '70s. Like many other countries, China requires instruction in the international language of business – English – as a second language (ESL).

So the Chinese don't have a choice, but you do. In fact, you have more than a choice – you have a strategic opportunity.

Here are the highlights of this chapter on language:

- If you were one of the early Westerners to go to China after it reopened in the '70s, you wouldn't recognize the China of today. After Nixon left, the early business entrepreneurs had a much more difficult time getting around, because no one in China spoke English. If they got into a taxi at the airport, unable to speak Mandarin, they wouldn't get two blocks out. They needed translators for everything.

- China changed dramatically as it worked to become a major world power. Today your taxi driver at the airport, even though he may be relatively uneducated, will at least speak some rudimentary English -- certainly enough to get you to your hotel. And, there's a pretty good chance that he'll be able to carry on a spirited discussion of any topic you'd care to bring up.

- In China's current educational system, most students take English as a second language.

- As a visitor to China, you can anticipate that the Chinese will be eager to practice their English with you.

- The Western presence is evident in China not only via the English spoken there, but also because of the American global brands that you'll see in every major city: Starbucks, McDonalds, Dunkin Donuts, Pizza Hut, etc. (Remember Indiana Tom from our first chapter, though – these American staples may be prepared differently enough that you won't recognize their familiar tastes and textures).

- In the corporate world of Chinese companies expanding outside of their home territory, English has become a mandatory skill. That's a dramatic change in just one generation. Twenty years ago, it was not mandatory for expats to speak English, so they routinely ventured west without language skills, and stuck even closer to each other than they do now.

- Today, all Chinese applicants for foreign postings are required to take a language proficiency test. Of course, this requirement doesn't apply to very connected individuals at the senior levels – they could probably get by with a multilingual staff.

- For those from the older generation who somehow missed English language instruction, trying to catch up now would be very difficult. Languages truly are best learned while young.

- For the Chinese trying to learn English – especially for those trying to learn as adults – have some empathy, because the international language of business doesn't translate all that well. Example: English has certain sounds, notably the "r" sound – that don't have an easy Mandarin equivalent. "Rock and roll" becomes "lock and loll" – not just in bad old movies, but in the everyday speech of Chinese people trying to converse in English.

- English doesn't have the layered tones, or pronunciations, that the Chinese dialects do. In Mandarin, each character has four different tones. In Cantonese, each has eight different tones. Can you imagine the challenge for those who are hard of hearing? A word pronounced incorrectly because of tone may have a completely different meaning.

- There's a big difference between proficiency and fluency. For Chinese expats working in the West, English proficiency is desired, but fluency is not required. Remember, your Chinese expat colleagues are likely to keep to themselves, and in their inner circles they will be speaking Chinese.

- For Westerners at Chinese-owned businesses, there are strategic advantages if you're perceived as not being proficient. Think about it: the Chinese are an inward-looking people, now confronted with Westerners in their midst. If they think you can't understand them, they'll probably say a lot more around you than if they think you understand every word.

- Think the last point forward a little bit: do you think some Westerners in Chinese-owned companies hide their proficiency? Hmm... Well, we'll say this: we do know of some Westerners who picked up more information by not letting on what they knew than the more established information-gathering techniques of listening to "private" conversations on airplanes, or in elevators, or in the little gems gleaned from the documents people leave on copy machines!

- It's probably easier for a Chinese adult to learn English than for an English adult to learn Chinese. For a middle-aged bureaucrat on either side, it'll be hard. We're aware of more than a few Westerners who tried – private lessons and all – then did a quick cost-benefit analysis and bagged it.

- For Chinese expats who go West and aren't already conversant, it's especially hard to gain fluency because they live in such sheltered quarters. They really can get by with very minimal English, beyond what they had to display on their proficiency test – the majority of their conversations in the office, plus emails, plus memos, plus everything they say at home – can easily happen in Chinese.

- If they want to, Chinese expats in the West have another way to avoid spoken or written English. The preferred clients of Chinese expats are other Chinese expats (though there might be a "Big Nose" or two around for cover).

- For Americans, foreign language is mostly an elective in schools. Does that display a kind of arrogance around this country's role as a world leader? The answer seems obvious to us.

- In some American communities, parents have a novel option: foreign language charter schools begin at kindergarten. Children become truly multi-lingual as a natural part of their education.

- Chinese expats don't typically put their kid in foreign language charter schools. Most expect their single child will remain though college, and believe it's best for the children to be immersed in English at school, and learn Chinese at home – but, as we've noted, children often rebel against the latter.

- You may wonder how Chinese expat parents think their child will be able to stay in the States through college. Well, parents here on a work visa can usually get on a green card track. Or, if the parents do go back to China, they'll send their child to an American boarding school. Student visas are pretty easy to get. Remember, Chinese parents have a ferocious focus on their single child, so they've probably prepared for this well in advance of leaving China in the first place.

- If by chance you're working in a Chinese-owned

NEVER TRY TO DRINK A CHINESE WOMAN UNDER THE TABLE

company with very few Western employees (or if you're the only one), you can expect that many or most meetings will be conducted in Chinese, with little or no translation. You'll spend a lot of time sitting and smiling. Your Chinese colleagues will translate if they have a question for you.

- In a meeting at a Chinese company, if there are two or more non-Chinese speakers, there will more of an attempt to conduct some of the meeting (and business in general) in English. It's not uncommon for meetings to flip back and forth between English and Mandarin.

- Here's our "We're Not China-Bashing Reminder": it's always easier for native speakers to speak their native language. This is not particular to the Chinese. It's natural and human nature.

- While it's very difficult and takes a long time to gain a working knowledge of Chinese, it can be very useful to understand at least a rudimentary set of business words. You'll pick it up over time, almost by osmosis.

- At Chinese companies, some English words are used because they don't have a literal translation.

- Even if you don't understand a word of the language, remember it's important as a colleague to watch people speaking and to listen. All the research says that most communication is non-verbal anyway. Pay attention to the tone of voice, expressions, who's speaking the most, who is deferred to, etc. You'll get a general sense of what is happening.

- Here's our favorite: Chinese is a loud language. Don't mistake a loud voice for an angry voice. Not just men, either: women are also full-voiced. What look (and sound) like screaming matches are common. How fun is that?

CASE STUDY

Join us now for "The Tale of Tim and Tom: Two Americans Who Looked Exactly the Same But Had Really Different Experiences at a Chinese-Owned Company."

Both Tim and Tom were hired by a Chinese electronics developer, New Sun Industries, in the San Francisco Bay Area.

They look like brothers. They're broad-shouldered, blonde, engaging, and fun to be around in a spent-formative-time-in-a-fraternity kind of way. Really, they're great guys. Tim and Tom both graduated from Stanford as undergrads, then went on immediately for their MBAs.

Neither targeted a Chinese company for their first job after finishing their MBAs, but they were aggressively recruited (along with many other classmates – New Sun was keen on establishing itself as an international powerhouse), and decided to take the job offers. During their interview process, both indicated that they had some exposure to Mandarin during their educations, as might be expected at a prestigious university like Stanford.

But here's where the ships part ways: Tim, son of a lovely Nordic family that settled in San Francisco generations ago, sort of paid attention in a language class he had to take in his junior year. Tom looked just like Tim, so probably also descended from Scandinavians.

Ah, but Tom was adopted. He's never met his birth parents. His adoptive parents include a father who was born in San

Francisco, and a mother who was born in Hong Kong.

Tim's one glancing classroom experience was the only acquaintance he ever made in Mandarin, with the possible exception of the pretty girl in class who let him copy from her exams (so he could pass the course). They actually dated for a short while.

Tom probably had about as much interest in the Chinese language as Tim, but his Hong Kong-born mother had other ideas. She insisted on a Chinese language school every Saturday from the time he was five through high school. At times he hated her for it, but he did make some pretty good friends over the course of his lessons. And he learned Chinese. [Tim knew none of this.]

But Tom put his foot down when he won admission to Stanford. No more Chinese lessons. He understood the language well enough, could converse with his Mom (especially when she shared secrets about his Dad), and was an adult capable of making his own decisions.

Time flies, Tim and Tom are hired and begin their jobs as business analysts at New Sun. They're in a lot of meetings where the predominant language is Chinese. Tim is lost, and does his best to fake some level of interest.

Just like riding a bike, all those weekend lessons come back to the other blonde man in our story, and he can actually understand most of what is being said. Tom does have trouble with some of the more technical concepts, and writes notes to review with his Mom.

"Are you going to let them know you know?" she asks on

the phone.

"What do you mean?" he counters.

"Maybe it's best, at least early on, to pay attention, but not participate," she says. "Sometimes less is more. You can learn more by listening than talking."

Tom has had his differences with his Mom, but has learned to listen to experts. She knows the culture. He has a working fluency of the written and spoken language. He decides to follow her advice.

Time goes by. Tim gets some sense of what's going on, based on the meager amount of business communications that are translated into English for him. He does passable work.

Tom soaks it all up, and whatever he doesn't understand his Mom translates for him. He can pick up whatever is being said at meetings. More importantly, because his Chinese colleagues don't know about his facility with their language, they talk freely in groups where he and Tim are present. Tim is clueless, but Tom learns who's who and what's what and where the opportunities are.

You can write the ending, can't you?

Tim lasts about six months at New Sun. He's bright, but doesn't have the patience to pay attention to all the non-verbal cues around him. And, he has no intention of taking Chinese language courses to catch up. We will credit Tim with one thing: he knows a losing situation when he sees one, and gets out. We've seen people go years and years before reaching the same conclusion (but, to be fair, they were making a lot more money than Tim was).

And, Tom? He rides the waves at New Sun, learns to impress the correct people, keeps his head down, and gets a promotion at about the same time that Tim accepts a new job (hoping to quickly erase this six-month mistake on his resume). Tom's future is bright, and always has the option to reveal a developing facility with his colleagues' language. Or not.

Our favorite person in this story is Tom's Mom. She gets complete validation for making him give up his Saturdays for language instruction, has become his chief professional confidant, and now can chide Tom's father that perhaps it's time that he learn a little Chinese, too!

LANGUAGE LESSONS

Even if you don't have a wise Mom who insisted you spend your childhood Saturdays taking Chinese language lessons, you can still have a leg up on your competition by understanding the role of language in Chinese business.

Here are the lessons to keep in mind:

1. Chinese expats who come west have to pass an English language proficiency test.

2. Westerners who work for Chinese companies do not have to pass a Mandarin proficiency test.

3. Westerners who work for Chinese companies, and do have a proficiency in Mandarin, should think carefully as to whether they want to reveal their knowledge, because....

4. Chinese colleagues will very naturally talk to each other in their native language. If they think a Westerner in their midst doesn't have a clue as to what they're saying, they're likely to say more.

5. The best time to learn a foreign language is when you're young, at the same time that you're learning your native language.

6. For the non-young, it's probably tougher for someone

who speaks English to learn Chinese than vice-versa.

7. As a Westerner, you're probably going to have to pick up at least some familiarity with basic Chinese business terms.

8. Even if you don't understand the predominant language, remember that most communication is non-verbal. You can learn a lot by listening to tone, emphasis, volume, and how people relate to each other.

9. English is the universal language of business, which explains why English is so popular at Mainland schools.

10. Chinese can be a really loud language. What will appear to be two Chinese businesspeople literally screaming at each other is just the way they talk and not any indication of hostility.

SIDEBAR:

What Did You Say?

Most countries in Asia require some level of English instruction both because English is the closest thing we have to an international language, and America is such a predominant leader in pop culture.

It's also our understanding that expats from many Asian cultures tend to stick to themselves when posted in a foreign country, which is one way they can keep their culture and traditions alive while they're away from home.

Okay, we admit it, we're suckers for a good story. Have you ever gotten in a jam over mishearing or misreading something while working for an Asian-owned company, or while traveling in Asia on business? We've already heard the "chicken flied lice" stories, so you 've gotta do better than that – and, as always, extra points if what you have to say is both culturally sensitive and funny!

Please, ahem, "talk" to us on our blog:

Never Try to Drink a Chinese Woman Under the Table [Plus Other Fun and Practical Tips] www.nevertrythis.net

FEAR OF FLIGHT:

The Passport Paradox

NEVER TAKE YOUR FREEDOMS as an American or Westerner for granted. Here's what we mean: if you had the money and the time, would you think twice about a long weekend outside the country? London, Paris, or Berlin? Just take your luggage and passport to the airport, and off you go, right?

Your Chinese expat colleagues don't have that option. They aren't allowed to keep their own passports. They have to turn them over as soon as they arrive at a posting outside of Mainland China. If they want to go away for a pleasure trip, they have to seek special permission, and their odds of getting it would depend on who they know.

As with all things, what we call The Passport Paradox is a direct reflection of the larger Chinese culture. Here are the highlights:

- Our specific focus in this chapter is expats from

Mainland China, who work for state-controlled businesses in the West (or anywhere else outside of China). We understand the situation may be similar for expats from Vietnam.

- This situation affects a lot of people, because most Chinese-owned businesses of any significant size are state-controlled (and controlled).

- We're including this chapter not as specific advice for you, but more so that you can understand some of pressures your Chinese colleagues face. This would not be your reality if you accept a posting abroad. Be thankful for that.

- This information is not really relevant to expats from Japan, South Korea, or any other Asian country that we know of, with the possible exception of Vietnamese expats because they also live under a totalitarian regime. Other Asian expats have home governments which are more democratic, and not as concerned with control issues.

- For Mainland Chinese expats working in United States or another country, their passports are collected as soon as they enter the foreign nation. Someone from their traveling party is usually assigned to collect and hold the passports.

- Similarly, when Chinese expats travel on business to other countries, as soon as they clear Immigration, their passports will be collected – again, usually by someone who is traveling with the group.

- You could joke with your Chinese expat colleagues that they shouldn't get too fond of their passport pictures, because they sure don't get much of a chance to see them. Um – second thought – don't. Probably not a good topic for humor.

- Fear of Flight is a reflection of the larger Chinese culture. There's an overriding concern, at the upper Communist party level, that some expats will jump ship if given the opportunity.

- The higher-ups aren't concerned about political defections as much as they are about economic ones: that life is simply better in the West (or perceived to be better). This was more the attitude 10 or 20 years ago than it is now, because economic conditions have vastly improved for China's middle and upper classes at home. But it's still guiding the political and business culture.

- Here's another sign that things are changing, at least back in China: businesses sometimes have trouble finding people who want to go west for several years. Pay back in China has gone up, and going abroad is a major hassle no matter how you cut it.

- Along with the cultural influences, Fear of Flight is also family-based. Expat families typically spend about six years in foreign postings (reflecting visa restrictions), and that's certainly enough time to start a family. Expat families in America often find their children become so acclimated that they don't want to go back, and also resist speaking or learning Mandarin at home. If they do go back, the kids will probably lose a year in school, because of the differences between Western and Chinese educational systems (and we stress that the systems are "different," not necessarily more or less advanced than others).

- Over the six-year course of a foreign posting, if an expat Chinese spouse has been able to find some sustaining work in the West, he or she (but probably she) may stay behind while the other major breadwinning spouse returns home or goes to another foreign posting.

- There have been cases where expats have gone on major spending or gambling sprees during their Western posting, and don't want to return home. They made – or lost – so much money that they can't hide it.

- Chinese expats in the West often set up investment accounts, and try to grow assets as much as they can. When they go home, they probably won't be able to take much of a financial windfall with them – that would be suspect. They could use it in the West, though, for their children's education.

- This will sound contradictory (and it is, which is why we love doing business with the Chinese), but there actually is more freedom to travel now. And, the children of Chinese parents in the U.S. may be able to spend some of the money their parents have worked so diligently to save. See how this dovetails with the Chinese love of shopping? It doesn't all go to books and tuition.

- Until about 15 years ago, it was required that the expat go west alone. The spouse and child stayed home. As difficult as it seems, it is not unusual today in China for a husband and wife to be geographically separated because they each have good jobs in different cities within China. The grandparents raise the child. Same thing happens on the international scale: sometimes the expat goes west alone these days, not because of any government requirement, but because the spouse may have a good job back in China.

- The relative level of freedom for Chinese expats is sort of elastic. If a more repressive regime comes to power, the grip tightens.

- When it's time to go home, expats are personally escorted to the airport, given their passports, and put on a plane.

CASE STUDY

Have you ever purchased a movie on DVD with multiple endings (typically one the director wanted in addition to the one the evil studio executives mandated)? Our case study is going to give you some differing ending options, so see if you can figure out how it will end.

Quin Ming is a successful mid-level officer for a Chinese internet company. His employer is looking to expand its international presence, and wants Ming to accept a foreign posting in the United States to implement the strategy. The company already has an office in New York, so he'll have an established base of operations.

Mr. Quin is excited at the prospect of living in New York and connecting with its vibrant online community. Also, he calculates that this high-profile assignment will be good for his career.

He arrives at New York's JFK airport after a long flight from the Mainland. He's met right outside of Customs by a local delegation of his new colleagues, who formally greet him and assure him that they will help in his transition to the always-bustling environment of New York City.

One member of the delegation requests Ming's passport, which he dutifully supplies. He had already received word that surrendering his government papers was standard operating procedure. Mr. Quin also knew that housing arrangements have already been made for him. Ask anyone who has ever tried to find an apartment in New York: nightmare! An apartment waiting for you upon arrival sounds great, but....

But Ming's new home is a small apartment building where all of his colleagues from Mainland China also live, along with employees of a few other Chinese-owned companies. Easier to keep an eye on each other, wouldn't you say? The building is owned by a Mainland Chinese investment company. All in the family.

Quin Ming actually likes the company, both at work and at home. New York can be a very overwhelming place for newcomers, and it's a comfort to be around people with a similar background and worldview.

Work takes all of his time. He's a constant presence at the office, and goes out with his new colleagues three to four nights a week for business events. Ming enjoys his colleagues, but does start to feel homesick.

After six months, his wife Kailai and son Bo join him in New York. He meets them at JFK, along with others from work. You already know what happens right after Customs – two new passports are added to the collection.

Everyone's charmed that Bo already speaks a bit of English. His mother had been tutoring him. He's five years old, and is immediately enrolled by his parents in a local public kindergarten.

Kailai is a quiet but modern woman, determined to create a career opportunity for herself while the family is in New York. She applies to and is accepted at a nursing school, thrilled that in two years she'll have a degree.

Let's fast forward through those two years. Kailai now has a job as a nurse with the New York public school system. Bo loves living here, has made many friends, and is now in the second grade. He doesn't like speaking Mandarin at home, and openly rebuffs his parents' attempts at a bilingual household. In private, they discuss this growing problem. What will they do when it's time to return home?

In the business world, Quin Ming's reputation is growing at the rate of a successful internet start-up. Everyone loves him, and he's making great contacts in the New York online community (and more than a few people in California like him too). The head office back in China concurs, especially since Ming has been able to meet and surpass the unrealistic targets for the New York office. Of course, he maintains a public face of humility and deference.

Let's move forward in the time machine. It's now Year Five. The Quin family is still in the same apartment building, just down the hall from Quin Ming's office colleagues and other Chinese expats. They were allowed to switch to a larger apartment when another family moved back to China, but didn't even consider moving to another building. Didn't even consider asking. Never entered their minds.

One Thursday afternoon in Year Five, Mr. Quin gets word from the headquarters office that his family's New York City stay will end in three months. A successor will arrive a few weeks before his departure to facilitate a smooth transition.

Ming's new American friends and business contacts are aghast: how can he leave? They love him! He's the face of the business! And his son is such a whiz on the soccer field!

Okay, we're at the point of offering three alternate endings, but before we do, let's issue a reminder that the Chinese are gracious people. No matter what happens, there will be a lovely banquet at a beautiful Manhattan restaurant (with authentic Chinese cuisine, of course) to honor Ming and his many New York accomplishments. He tells his colleagues how much he will miss them, and that he will of course stay in touch – his new position at the company will have some global responsibilities.

So, Ming is going out on a high note. Or is he? Here are three options:

1. The Quins pack up their apartment, somehow convince Bo that going to Beijing will be a great new adventure, and head to the airport with a work delegation. They are given their passports, go through Immigration and Security, get on a plane, and fly home to begin the next chapter of their lives as a family – a family that decided to stay together.

2. Anticipating that this time would come, and knowing that Bo would rather hurl himself off a bridge than go to China, Kailai secures a work visa – sponsored by the New York public school system – that will allow her to stay in the country for another four years. Quin Ming heads home, leaving his wife and son behind. He will do his best to stay in touch, will see them when he can, and may soon inquire about another foreign posting somewhere in the Western Hemisphere. Maybe Latin America?

3. Same as Number Two, at least as far as Ming's colleagues know: he's going home, while the wife and

son are staying here. His colleagues take him to the airport, hand over his passport, and watch while he enters the Immigration line. Satisfied that he's headed to the plane, they return to the office.

Ming waits a few minutes after his colleagues depart, then turns around, walks back into the main terminal, and leaves the airport. He joins his wife on Manhattan's Upper West Side, where they have already rented a new apartment.

The next Monday, Ming will report to his new job at an American internet company – a company which has already been in contact with a local congressional office to help arrange for a green card due to Ming's advanced technical capabilities and obvious value. Bo is thrilled that both parents will be there to watch as he starts a new soccer season.

Ming's colleagues will be blamed for letting him get away, and will be faced with censure at best or perhaps demotion or other disciplinary measures – like being sent home for "political reeducation." Ming feels bad about that, and hopes he'll be able to clear the slate with his former colleagues sometime in the near future. But the decision was relatively easy for him: family first. A big "ouch" for everyone else.

So, which scenario do you pick? Perhaps it would help to know how likely each outcome might be. In our experience, options one and two happen all the time. Three is a rare occurrence.

By the way, in order to get away with Number Three, the Quins would have to be pretty good actors. If anyone of their colleagues thought something was up, then someone from the office would've been assigned to accompany him back to China.

FEAR OF FLIGHT LESSONS

Bit of a whirlwind, don't you think? Can you imagine the amount of coordination involved in actually pulling off Option Three: getting out of the apartment with at least some of their belongings, making colleagues think a return to China was about to happen, and giving no one (in a community where everyone keeps an eye on everyone else) any reason to think that something was up. Sort of strikes us as a decent subplot for an upcoming James Bond 007 movie!

Here are the lessons to keep in mind:

1. Expats from Mainland China have to deal with conditions unlike almost any other business people contemplating a foreign posting.

2. Passports are collected from Chinese expats when they arrive in the West to work for a state-controlled company.

3. Almost every Chinese-owned business of any size is state-controlled.

4. Chinese culture explains how the Passport Paradox got started. The Chinese are a consensus-oriented people, and tend to stick together in foreign countries.

5. China's government and political elite have maintained

the restrictions, which are based more on economics than current reality. The difference between living conditions in China vs. the West used to be quite stark; they are less so now.

6. Chinese expats not only have to give up their passports upon arrival in the West, they're also likely to live in very close proximity to other expats, which encourages not only community but everyone keeping an eye on each other.

7. Family pressures weigh on Chinese expats. A six-year posting allows enough time to start a family, and for a spouse to develop an independent career. It can be very difficult to uproot a family – after a foreign posting – to return to China.

8. Chinese expats often invest their money while living abroad. Taking a lot of money home is suspect, so earnings may end up getting spent in the West – sometimes on education for the children, and sometimes for frivolous things.

9. The end of a foreign posting can come quickly for a Chinese expat. There's an incentive to make advance arrangements for the spouse and child, especially if they want to stay behind.

10. Most expats are fully compliant with returning the breadwinner to China as ordered, but exceptions do happen.

SIDEBAR:

What if You're Not a Chinese Expat?

We were very careful to focus this chapter only on expats from Mainland China who accept a foreign posting. Our goal was to give you a sense of the pressures that your Chinese colleagues face, though their situation is one you will probably never have to deal with personally.

We also mentioned Vietnamese expats, because it's our understanding that they face similar pressures and procedures, reflecting that they too come from a totalitarian state.

But, how about everyone else? Do you have expat colleagues from other Asian countries who face scrutiny unique to their home cultures and politics? If so, how did you learn about it? Are these restrictions open knowledge, or did you hear about them only after years of building trust?

Please let us know about it on our blog:

Never Try to Drink a Chinese Woman Under the Table
[Plus Other Fun and Practical Tips]
www.nevertrythis.net

GOING SOLO VS. GROUP THINK:

Americans are Lone Wolves; the Chinese are Pack Animals

HAVE YOU EVER WATCHED kids play in a sandbox? Think about it as we make a few opening observations about a profound difference between the Chinese and American cultures.

Everyone, across cultures, wants their child to get along with the other kids in the sandbox. For one thing, fights are messy and someone ends up with sand in his shoes (not to mention his underwear).

Let's push the analogy a little bit: in China, the whole

culture operates like a sandbox. Everyone is expected to not only get along, but make mutual, consensus decisions about the games that will be played. No obvious winners or losers.

You know how different the American sandbox is. Yes, everyone is expected to play nice and observe basic rules like not kicking other kids or eating sand. But, in the American sandbox, you'll often observe a nerdy kid who plays by himself – he's probably trying to figure out how much better this sandbox would work if it were completely reconfigured. That kid will probably have a tough childhood, but will grow into a Gates or a Jobs or a Buffett and become a billionaire.

American culture celebrates lone wolves. China abhors them. Here are the points we'd like to highlight in this chapter:

- First off, a personal reflection from Richard: when he first started working for the Chinese decades ago, he firmly believed the Chinese would take over the world, and that the United States was in decline. But, after gaining experience in how the Chinese do business compared to Americans, he changed his mind and now believes the U.S. really has very little reason to be afraid. The Chinese produce the goods, but it's the Americans who have the ideas – not because of any innate differences between the races, but because each race has a culture and history that explains the way its members operate.

- The U.S. education system is probably unique in the world in that it is based on individual thought and the creation of ideas – which is why students from all over the world come here. Of those who come from China, many don't go back. American education is their ticket out.

- The Chinese education system is based on rote memorization, the accumulation of facts, and the ability to regurgitate those facts. This has very little to do with being able to solve problems. The current Chinese system is highly valued by its Communist Party, since above all it teaches Chinese citizens to follow the rules. If someone for whatever reason develops the ability to think independently, do you see how that could be perceived as dangerous in China's totalitarian culture?

- The Chinese educational system is complemented by cultural indoctrination. In school, within families, on television, and in sports groups, the message of conformity is reinforced over and over again. What a contrast with the U.S. mindset, which teaches individuals to strive, chase their dreams, be creative, come up with novel solutions, and learn the rules so you can break them. The obvious result is a strong entrepreneurial system – and the guys who really succeed, like Gates and Jobs and Buffett – become cultural icons.

- A successful manager in the U.S. if often going to be an idea generator, who fosters creativity, finds solutions, understands what's broken and fixes it, and mentors employees. [Okay, caveat, we've all worked in crappy places that operate quite differently than this ideal. Still it is the American cultural ideal.]

- In business as in life, the Chinese have a very clearly

defined structure. Starting at the bottom, people who are "doing the work" are virtual automatons. They're told what to do, they follow instructions, and they seldom question anything. In the States, this happens in only the most traditional and mechanized industries – certainly not among today's creative outliers who go mainstream after they succeed.

- The Chinese system fosters fraud and corruption to a much greater degree than its Western counterparts. If workers are taught not to question, but only follow instructions, great power accrues to those at higher levels. Since goals are usually set in the stratosphere and therefore unattainable, everyone cooks the numbers. Ronald Reagan wasn't so far off when he said trust, but verify (although he was talking about Russians and not the Chinese).

- American regulators often force accountability on Chinese-owned businesses in the States – notably in financial services.

- It's human nature to a certain extent to stretch the truth and see what you can get away with. But in the U.S., those who do so run the risk of being prosecuted. It's a very different regulatory and legal environment in China.

- There's an active revolving door between Chinese government and state-controlled industries (which includes most businesses of any real size and importance). In both, there is very little wiggle room for individual leaders to do anything groundbreaking or novel. They need the support and approval of comrades.

Today's mayor of a city can become tomorrow's head of a steel mill, and individuals have no choice in the matter – you're told where you're going next.

- A Chinese success is always reflective of the group – both in politics and government.

- If a Chinese individual is singled out for success, he or she will often try to deflect it, and to make it about the group. Accepting individual praise is often tantamount to painting a big red bulls eye on your back.

- Even at the most senior levels of Chinese business and government, everyone worries about their connections, and spends an endless amount of time tending to them.

- At least in public, Chinese leaders are very self-effacing. But, it would be a mistake to equate their public faces with their private conduct. Power mongers and insufferable suck-ups are everywhere.

- You do have public moguls (i.e., Donald Trump) in China. But, they do not work for state-controlled companies, and do not allow themselves to become media stars. They work as hard as anyone to make sure that their friends are taken care of. China's new capitalists all curry favor.

- China's new capitalists – the country's new wealth – have mastered an unwritten rule book of how to be financially and corporately successful without incurring the wrath of political leaders at local and higher levels. They know that if their political contacts aren't tended properly, they can be charged with misdeeds. As an aside, the situation is much less discreet in Russia to the north, where multi-billionaires have gone to jail for crossing the government.

- Time to step back for a second, because we think a lot of the Chinese experience is basic human nature, albeit honed over many years of cultural indoctrination. People want to share in a good thing, see that their friends are taken care of, in hopes that everyone prospers (albeit some more than others).

- Since China's "Great March Forward," the whole political and social structure has been built on "Group Think" – or, more accurately – "Group Non-Think." Creativity is often deemed dangerous in the business world.

- China's entrepreneurial business culture is much more driven by economics than creativity. You're not going to find a Steve Jobs in China. The Chinese Steve Jobs will come to Stanford to study. He'll create a business empire in the West, and might eventually open a branch in China. He won't put his headquarters there, because it wouldn't be successful.

- The key to China's business success has been its ability to serve as a low-cost provider.

- Don't be fooled by the idea of "A New China." It's usually just smart PR, and involves China being praised by its paid Western consultants.

- Power in China flows from government control over its people – and certainly has historical roots, with a vast agrarian system that required the diligent labor of the masses. But especially since the days of Mao, power is never vested in the hands of one person. There is an upper echelon – the Central Committee – with all the palace intrigue you might expect.

- Circling back, the Chinese system starts with its children, and with an educational system built around a belief in the superiority of the group over the individual. A liberal arts education is almost exclusively a Western (and especially American) way to promote individual creativity.

- From time to time in modern China, you will see business and government leaders try to adopt Western methods. You'll know that they've gone too far when rumors start appearing against them – a sure sign of their initial fall from grace. More serious punishment often follows.

- Within the Chinese Communist Party structure, there is a senior person in charge of party discipline. It's a very powerful position.

- To maintain discipline, the Chinese have a massive re-education system. Troublemakers are sent away to "camp" – depending on the level and severity of the transgression, it could be an intensive school-like setting. Or, it could literally be a prison. Rehabilitation is possible, though the course of reeducation can take upwards of a year.

- At the Party level, there is ongoing education – and this includes expats working at Chinese-owned companies in the West. Periodically, Chinese workers in places like New York City and San Francisco are gathered for political education. It can take the form of webcasts, addresses by high-level executives, or presentations by visitors from China. Participation is mandatory, and crucial for career advancement. An invitation to join the Party is coveted, and real success means signing on to everything.

- The "brainstorming" so common in Western business really doesn't happen in Chinese-owned businesses. Brainstorms allow individuals to shine for their creative ideas and novel ways of thinking. As we've indicated, that's just not the way things go in Chinese culture and within the Chinese business mindset.

CASE STUDY

Remember the sandbox at the start of this chapter? You would've noticed Peter Douglas in it. He organized the other kids to help build a sandcastle. All the observant mothers thought he was the cutest thing they'd ever seen. Peter's Mom thought so too.

He lived a charmed adolescence in suburban Connecticut: popular at school, excelled in every subject he cared enough to study for. We could throw in homecoming king and quarterback, but that would pull us into gag-worthy territory.

Let's just say Peter Douglas was a great kid with a bright future.

After graduating from New York University's Stern School of Business with his MBA, Peter accepted a job as an entry-level manager with a Chinese-owned transportation firm in New York City. Calm Seas Industries focused on long-distance shipping, notably between Western ports and China – raw materials into the home country, finished products exported abroad.

Frankly, Calm Seas wasn't on Peter's list of dream jobs. They offered the most money, and he wanted to put his debt behind him as quickly as possible. Also, he was fascinated by Asia, and thought Calm Seas might provide opportunities to travel. Calm Seas' recruiter implied it would.

Peter spent his first six months as a diligent, attentive, respectful junior manager. He was a personable guy, and very bright, and quickly mastered whatever work came his way.

One day Peter took some initiative in his junior management work group, and pointed out a significant inefficiency in Calm Seas' methods of refueling its tanker fleet. He proposed a fix that could save the company significant budget in its annual energy costs.

The idea was a hit. It made obvious sense to the American office's bottom line, and actually helped it to exceed the home office's expectations for the year.

Peter expected a reward, some recognition of the sort he received in business school for his leadership of projects and insightful analysis.

But here's where Peter Douglas goes south. If he had made such a big-dollar improvement at a Western company, a significant promotion and pay raise would very likely be his. Perhaps even stock options.

But Peter wasn't working for a Western fleet owner. Calm Seas was a state-controlled Chinese business operating in the West. There was some level of acknowledgement for the productivity gain, but when it was finally attributed (months after the fact); it was simply noted as an achievement of the North American division and its management team.

Privately, Peter's superiors were mostly heartened that they were able to exceed the home office's budget expectations for the fourth quarter without fudging the numbers. Peter, and everyone else at his level, received identical pay raises and bonuses.

Peter managed to join in on a group trip to the home office

in Beijing, and made the obligatory visit to the Great Wall. Knowing that his future was not at Calm Seas, he started contacting recruiters as soon as he got back.

That's not quite the end of the story. There was another Peter hired the same day as Peter Douglas. Peter Chin was the son of Beijing-based parents, who were also thrilled that their son had graduated with a prestigious U.S. MBA (they certainly paid enough for it) and landed a job at Calm Seas. They did have a few relatives with connections that put in a good word with the hiring managers.

Peter Chin was as book-smart as Peter Douglas, with just as many great ideas, but he was also a student of Chinese culture, learned from his doting parents. They taught him deference and consensus-oriented social skills. While Peter Douglas was coming up with ideas that would make him stand out, Peter Chin was focused on fitting in – being always and instantly available for his superiors, driving visitors from China on their shopping trips, and socializing with his new Chinese colleagues.

Peter Douglas is now on a management track at a different U.S.-owned company. He's the star at company brainstorms with his creative and innovative ideas.

Peter Chin has received two promotions with accompanying bonuses at Calm Seas. His future within Chinese-owned businesses couldn't be brighter.

See how it can work out both ways?

GROUP THINK LESSONS

Other than the obvious point that Peter could have saved himself a few years – and traveled to the Great Wall on his own dime – if only he had read this book, let's review the lessons of this chapter:

1. Americans are lone wolves. Historically and culturally, Americans are taught to develop creative, problem-solving capacity ... and to expect individual credit for their accomplishments.

2. The Chinese are pack animals. Historically and culturally, the Chinese are taught to conform to the consensus of groups ... and to deflect any individual credit for their own accomplishments.

3. In Western educational systems – and particularly in American schools – individual achievement and development are stressed.

4. The Chinese educational system is built around rote memorization of facts. Individual participation is expected, but the common focus is a group-oriented, control model.

5. In America, big individual personalities and talents are prized in the business and cultural arenas. These talents are often lushly rewarded with great treasure.

6. In China, it is possible for a cultural talent or business mogul to shine to some degree as an individual, but you are very likely to find Chinese entrepreneurial talent getting its education and early success in the West.

7. American business is certainly not immune to instances of fraud or corruption, but there is a general respect in the West for the rule of law and transparency.

8. China's government and state-controlled businesses are two stops on a constantly revolving door, and instances of graft are common and mostly understood as the cost of doing business and maintaining networks.

9. In America and other Western countries, business people may affiliate with one of the two major political parties, but it is far from mandatory.

10. In China, participation in party education, and re-education, are essential to career development.

SIDEBAR:

How Big is Your Sandbox?

It's our sense that the Chinese focus on Groupthink illustrated in this chapter lies at one end of the spectrum, while the American emphasis on the individual is at the other.

Further, it would follow that countries with governments and social structures similar to China's totalitarianism would land at similar place on the spectrum, while the Western democracies will largely clump together.

But we're also aware that the American liberal arts university education is fairly unique in the world. In most places, including other Western countries, advanced students go to college to learn a trade or specialization.

So where does your experience fit on the spectrum? If you grew up in Australia, but work in your native country for a Chinese-owned business, do the cultures complement or clash?

How about someone from Japan, who grew up under a Westernized monarchy? Would the experience of working for a Chinese-owned business be like parachuting into another world?

We love to hear stories. Please share yours on our blog:

Never Try to Drink a Chinese Woman Under the Table
[Plus Other Fun and Practical Tips]
www.nevertrythis.net

The Corporate Environment:

What to Expect INSIDE the Office

CLIMBING THE LADDER:

How High Can You Go?

Pop Quiz: There are five levels in the Chinese business hierarchy. As an American, are you closer to the top (Level 1) or the bottom (Level 5)?

Answer: you are Level 5. You're in this bunch whether you're of Irish descent living in Chicago, or an American-born Chinese (ABC).

The five levels of hierarchy that we've observed vary based on whether the individual is a native of the Chinese mainland, member of the Party, has family connections, went to a prestigious school, has appropriate experience, and age.

Let's review the five levels (and note that members of the higher groups typically travel on diplomatic passports):

Level 1 – Everyone here is a Chinese native, Party member, has family connections, went to a prestigious school in China, is now working as a senior executive, is more likely to be male, and is in the 45-60 age range (remember, most Chinese men in state-controlled businesses have a mandatory retirement age of 60). The U.S. equivalent? We don't mean to stereotype (too much), but think of the "Harvard MBA Country Club Blonde Handsome Executive Whose Grandfather Was a Senator." A young Robert Redford-type would play him in the film.

Level 2 – They're also Chinese natives, and were invited to join the Party, same as the Ones. What they don't have are family connections. Instead, they've nurtured relationships for years in their business work – meaning they gave freely of their time, always deferred to senior management and other superiors. The Twos are in the 40-60 age range. Level 2's U.S. equivalent? You know the guy in your company who's always first in, always last to leave? Always smiling? Always available?

Level 3 – The Threes are younger Chinese natives, age 28-40, and not necessarily Party members.

Level 4 – The Fours are Hong Kong-born Chinese. They can technically move into Level 2 senior executive positions, but will always be viewed with suspicion, never fully trusted, or involved in high-level decisions.

Level 5 – The Fives are Westerners, whether or not they speak Mandarin. Like the Fours, they can rise to Level 2 positions in title, but probably not in responsibility. They are most often figureheads who serve as window dressing. As we've already seen, ABCs (American Born Chinese) are in this group.

Sounds a little like high school, doesn't it: who's cool and who's not? In addition to the hierarchy, here's some points we want to stress:

- There's not much real difference between government/ Party and business, especially since so many of the large businesses are state-controlled. High-level managers do not need industry or product specialization.

- If they work in state-controlled companies, the government determines where individual Chinese will work and when their positions will change. Remember, all the major businesses are state-controlled, even if they're publicly-traded.

- Chinese government bureaucrats don't generally value expertise by industry. You can easily find someone at the top of a financial services conglomerate who doesn't know finance. He may have been a mayor or an executive in a totally different sector.

- Business gets done based on who you know rather than who you are (of course who you are determines who you'll get the opportunity to meet). Yep, we know ... the same thing is often said of American business.

- It's very unusual for someone to reach the premier level without growing up in an influential family with connections. Family and friends count more than brainpower.

- Retirement in China: 60 for men, 55 for women. The rules are looser for those in top level government positions – they can stay longer.

- There is real value in knowing Mandarin but not revealing that you do (see the chapter on Language).

There's also some risk.

- Compensation for Westerners in Chinese companies is comparable to industry standards. Extensive travel is not usually expected.

- In meetings, Westerners are usually vastly outnumbered by the Chinese. It's not uncommon for a visiting American salesperson to be seated in a room with 10 Chinese from the headquarters office. When the Chinese travel abroad, they always have a large delegation. If you expect to meet with two people, eight will show up.

- The Chinese hierarchy can be frustrating for Westerners at Chinese companies who are baffled at their inability to ascend the ladder. Here's the hard truth, as we've observed it: the rules are set, and reflect the Chinese culture. They're not open to change. No discussion. Accept that or go. It's important to understand your role and manage your expectations.

- If you're a Westerner taking a job with a Chinese company, don't be naïve. Your job title / description and your actual responsibilities may be quite different.

CASE STUDY

Through the eyes of an American hired by a Chinese-owned company, see if you can identify the different levels of Chinese business hierarchy...

Susan's claim to fame is that she just managed the rollout of a major new electronic product for an American manufacturer. She was looking for a new challenge, so she accepted the offer of a Chinese-owned company with a substantial salary increase. She would continue to be based in Los Angeles, and was gratified when her new employer issued a glowing press release announcing her hire to the LA business press. She has been told that her new job is to help expand business in the American market. If she were to look at our hierarchy chart, her responsibilities would suggest she's a Two (but you know she's really a Five with a Two job title).

Right out of the gate, Susan is warmly welcomed and invited to a number of lunches with mid- and upper-level managers. She hopes these meetings will allow her to learn more about her new employer and its culture (beyond the committee-approved description in the search firm's packet used while recruiting her). Susan wants to start on the right foot, and confirm that her job responsibilities are what she thinks they are. How American of her!

Here's an overview of the meetings, which took place over several weeks:

1. Mr. Li came to the States after several global postings

for another Chinese-owned company. His father-in-law was a top communist party official in Beijing, was instrumental in facilitating this placement, and is reportedly working on his son-in-law's next move – a return to China and a prestigious government post. Mr. Li is in his late 40's. He studied business at the prestigious Beijing University. He did not attend an MBA program at an American university. He understands spoken and written English, but is hesitant to speak it. His meeting with Susan is held in his office, and is not conducted over a meal. He is well-known in the company for trying to conduct business in a much less ritualized, more "Western Management by Objectives" featuring performance appraisals. Mr. Li was strongly supportive of the decision to hire Susan, and Susan knows that, so she feels some rapport with him. Her meeting with this Number One is completely professional and cordial, but Susan leaves somewhat uncertain as to what her real job might be. She thinks and hopes she'll have the support she needs.

2. Mr. Wu was invited to join the Party, but does not have family connections. He's spent his career working diligently as a mid-level bureaucrat – opening doors, carrying briefcases – and always available for "anything" that's needed (and, we mean anything). He's from Tianjin (about an hour away from Beijing). He speaks English fluently, and is in his late 40's. This was the hardest meeting to arrange because Mr. Wu's secretary kept calling to reschedule. Susan has heard that this Number Two doesn't like Americans and doesn't trust them, but she leaves his office with a completely opposite impression. Mr. Wu was gracious, relaxed,

and spoke in glowing terms about the company and his excitement at Susan's addition to the team. Susan couldn't sense it, and won't figure it out for months. Mr. Wu totally snowed her. He's an expert at hiding his true feelings.

3. Ms. Zhang is the supervisor of the Human Resources Department. A stylish woman in her late 30's from Shanghai, and a fluent English speaker, but she's not a Party member. Meeting with this Number Three is like reading an HR code of conduct book. Ms. Three does not once deviate from the company's approved policy or advice to new employees. She knows the rules by heart, having worked for the company for 15 years. For Ms. Zhang, it's all about following the rules. She would not think of sharing any current (and usually reliable) office gossip with a newcomer.

4. Okay, it should be obvious by now that we're sticking to the numbers. Our Number Four, Mr. Fung, was born, raised, and educated in Hong Kong before immigrating to the United States. Susan isn't sure of his title, but knows he's part of the general management team. Mr. Fung has spent more than 20 years with the company in Los Angeles. He takes her to lunch, and recites a useful history of the company over his two decades. Susan doesn't really talk. She leaves with the impression that he's accepted her, but also has a nagging suspicion that she needs to watch out for him.

5. Our Number Five is Joe. He's American-born, and does not speak Mandarin. He's the sole American, besides Susan, at a senior level. Joe joined the company 10

years ago, following a career of more than 30 years at industry-leading firms. As a consummate professional, he welcomes her to the company over lunch and spends the entire meeting helping her to understand the frustrations of not being Chinese: "Remember, you'll always be on the outside," he says.

Over the next six months, Susan's frustration builds. The one Chinese person she develops a good working relationship with is Mr. Liu (he's a senior-level manager responsible for accounting). They meet informally, one-to-one, and do manage to have some in-depth discussions (he speaks fluent English) which help her to gain some insight into the company's culture and politics.

Six months later, Mr. Liu reveals to Susan that the company's headquarters in Beijing is planning to send a high-level executive that she would report to. Susan now has a better understanding of this company and its culture. She starts talking with recruiters, and hands in her resignation as soon as she lands another job. It became increasingly clear to her that she couldn't achieve what she thought she was brought in to do, and was unwilling to place her career on hold in exchange for a fat paycheck. Her resignation is accepted without question.

What happened? They probably didn't want her in the first place. Mr. Li, our Number One, may not have had consensus to make a move forward. True, he's in charge, but that doesn't mean he had the power to both hire her and clear her path among the Number Twos, Threes, Fours and Fives.

One other possibility: they hired her just for the perceived image-building of the news release announcing her arrival, which received wide attention in the LA business press (and was quickly forwarded to headquarters back in China).

CLIMBING THE LADDER LESSONS

Feeling a little confused? That's common. Doing business with the Chinese, or working for a Chinese-owned company in the West can be both confusing and frustrating. So remember these:

1. It's not just a Chinese thing. Most people go with what they know. There are many distinct, though unwritten levels of power within a business – Chinese or Western.

2. It's very easy to misunderstand roles and responsibilities.

3. As discussed in "When does Yes Mean Yes," it can be very confusing to gauge your level of support for any initiative.

4. You need to explore in greater depth than in American companies what your specific role and job is.

5. Don't assume that your title is what it says.

6. There's a lot of value in building one-on-one relationships with people. It's possible to have discussions with people in levels Two and Three – but that trust is built over time. It's not necessarily support, but an information channel – which can be critical to survival.

7. Grab opportunities to have one-on-one meetings with

Asian colleagues. Meetings should not have an agenda, or any expectations. Develop rapport and trust first, and then see what happens.

8. The rumor mills in Chinese companies are much better developed than in American ones – and they're usually correct.

9. Information leaks are common. People are probably instructed to leak by their superiors.

10. You'll rarely see an organization chart. Even if you do, don't be taken in by it. It's just a chart, not how the power actually flows.

SIDEBAR:

Another Asian Business Hierarchy

We almost titled the preceding chapter "The Chinese Caste System," but made a change after it was suggested that we might be perceived as China-bashing (as you know by now, we mock and poke fun, but never bash).

Let's switch the focus to another country that is known historically for its caste structure, which we're told remains firmly in place in its business hierarchy: India.

We have friends who've done a lot of business with Indians, and here's what they tell us:

- India is the most hierarchical culture in the developed/ developing world. Decisions are made at the top, and superiors micromanage their staff.

- While it's always dangerous to generalize, most businesses are family-owned (and of course a family business is very different from an Indian subsidiary of a multinational corporation).

- Always try to deal with the most senior person in an organization. Those in the middle are just taking orders, and micromanaging those beneath them.

- Initiative from subordinates and contractors is not expected. They just do what they're told to do.

- Work teams expect exact instructions.

- Businesspeople will tell you what they think you want to hear.

- Positive feedback is prized, while "constructive criticism" is usually not.

- Meetings never start on time, and can ramble forever.

- Personal relationships are critical and build slowly over time.

Does all of this sound familiar to those of you who've done business in India? Since most of the Indian-owned businesses in the States are relatively small, we're assuming that a discussion of India is mostly about doing business there versus working for Indians here.

India is a fascinating country – bustling, crowded, and noisy. It's the most populous nation after China, and the world's most populous democracy. The economy is growing, and has become a major outsourcing destination with its educated population and relatively low wages. Indians commonly work 12-hour days, but the workplace is very social with many breaks.

What about other countries in Asia? We'd love to hear from you about the hierarchies in the workplace. We anticipate more evidence supporting our theory that you can't generalize the experience of one Asian country to the 50-plus others, but hey – you never know.

We love to hear stories. Please share yours on our blog:

Never Try to Drink a Chinese Woman Under the Table
[Plus Other Fun and Practical Tips]
www.nevertrythis.net

WHO'S TO BLAME?

The Art of Consensus

E VERYONE LIKES TO WIN; no one likes to fail. And we all have our culturally-influenced ways of doing things. Not better or worse, just different.

In China, it's been our observation that everyone is terrified of failure – in business, and in all other aspects of life as well (which may help explain the Chinese emphasis on excellence in education, national pride in the number of gold medals earned at the Olympics, and even an individual child's mastery of the piano to please her hovering parents).

When something goes wrong in Western business culture, there is usually an investigation to figure out what happened, prevent future occurrence, and look for long-term solutions.

In China, failure requires a scapegoat, because culture and tradition dictate that someone must be the personal receptacle of blame (and preferably just one person, at the lowest possible level in the organization). It's less about understanding why something went wrong and finding solutions than sweeping it under the rug with a scapegoat.

Here are the points we'd like to highlight:

- The Chinese place great emphasis on group decisions. In a typical Chinese-owned corporation, there are committees for everything.

- The Chinese are always looking over their shoulders. There's a saying we've heard a number of times: "It only takes three people. Two will be watching the other."

- Chinese expats working for state-controlled companies are generally not allowed to live where they want, especially in the United States. Small enclaves encourage community, and more importantly facilitate them keeping an eye on each other. In New York City, visiting Chinese business people are often required to stay at the Consulate (which was custom-built by a Chinese construction company).

- The higher you go within a Chinese-owned business, the more important it is that decisions are made at a group and not an individual level. This approach helps to protect individuals from being blamed later if something goes wrong. It's usually the practice to never leave a paper trail that can trace a decision to you as an individual. The Chinese tend to use the minimum documentation possible (including emails).

- Some people do get away with taking responsibility for their own decisions. They somehow are never punished for it, but they do make veterans of the consensus-driven business culture uncomfortable. And, if something ever does go seriously wrong, they risk being blamed.

- Before there is ever a committee meeting, there is lots of back-door lobbying and discussion. The theme is obvious – unanimity at all costs. Again, our advice is to always cover your back, and never leave yourself exposed to blame – unless you really enjoy taking risks (then of course you'd be more fun to have a drink with, at least as long as you last).

- Here's a term you may hear: "Flags of Blame." It literally means you get a colored flag, possibly in your personnel file, if you've done something that caused disfavor.

- Within a Chinese-owned company, it is common to detect general terror of not "properly" following instructions that come from the head office -- especially target budget and sales projections. No one questions anything, no matter how preposterous it might be. This of course leads to the production of less-than-honest reporting to the head office.

- Deadlines set by the head office are always unreasonably short. No one will ever challenge them. People will work late evenings and weekends to comply, even though the information is rarely, if ever, actually used.

- Beware the Chinese version of Catch-22: If you don't reach a target you're punished. If you do reach your target you haven't worked hard enough to exceed the

NEVER TRY TO DRINK A CHINESE WOMAN UNDER THE TABLE

target.

- The Blame Game permeates the culture within a Chinese-owned corporation. Everyone's first goal is to minimize their personal vulnerability. Any risky action has to be attributable to a group, and preferably a group at a lower level.

- The Chinese, when confronted with a problem, will say: "This is very serious. Who's to blame for this?" We've never seen anyone stand up and say, "This was my decision and my responsibility."

- Junior people assigned to take the blame on any individual matter can never confront their accusers, who are of course senior to them. They must be deferential.

- Do scapegoats have any options? They may try to get even. If they remain in the organization, they may seek vengeance by spreading dirt and starting rumors.

- A tried-and-true method of advancement in a Chinese company is to curry the favor of senior people. Aim for two or three levels above you, and try to anticipate their needs. This may sound a lot like the American mentor/ protégé relationship, but the Chinese version includes driving, making personal arrangements, keeping cups of tea filled, and satisfying whatever "special" need is presented.

- Senior business people are expected to have an entourage. They're never on their own. For a Chinese business person coming to the States, he or she (probably he) would never arrive at the airport without a waiting delegation to meet and drive him. No one takes airport taxis.

- What's important is what school you went to, who your parents are, and who you know. If you haven't got those things, you become a lackey to get rewarded.

- Expats are on call 24/7. They are not allowed to turn off their cell phones. There's very little concern for people's private lives. It's standard for people to have to cancel their vacations without reimbursement.

- "You work whenever we need you," is a basic mantra at a Chinese-owned company.

- The Chinese system of doing business is not necessarily a productive system; it's just that there are billions of people available to do jobs. We found it stunning to see people openly sleeping at their desks. They'd been there late into the night, and clearly got the message: "If you don't like it, we can easily replace you."

- The whole Chinese system is so powerful that individuality gets quashed. Their cultural training is similar to immersive religious training in the States.

- We have never seen the Blame Game not operational, or any suggestion of or interest in reform.

CASE STUDY

Let's put this together in a viable real-world situation. We'll set the stage at a major Chinese conglomerate looking to enter the U.S. market to secure a stable supply of junk metal.

The Chinese send eight people from Chengdu, a major city in Szechuan Province. They're a little bit rural, and do not have the sophistication of a group from Shanghai or Beijing. Of the eight, the six senior people are all in their late 40's or early 50's, and don't speak English. Two younger colleagues are university grads in their late 20's—they're on the trip to act as translators, assistants, and note-takers. [Note: The Chinese always provide their own translators, both in the U.S. and in China. They'd never trust someone they don't know to translate for them.]

It's everyone's first trip to America. Their destination: Chicago.

They're met by a group from the Chinese Consulate who are helping to organize their trip as well as a welcoming group from the Chicago Mayor's Office (very active in encouraging Asian business). They're in town for three days.

A two-year, no-cancellation deal is signed for a significant monthly shipment. Stand-by letters of credit are put in place as guarantees. The Chinese are very happy with the terms.

There's of course a huge banquet to celebrate the deal (see the chapters on food and alcohol). Everyone leaves happy.

After the group has returned to Chengdu, the relationship formally begins and the first shipment is scheduled in 30 days. The initial rollout is flawless; product is sent and received exactly corresponding to the terms of the agreement. Everything is fine for a few months, then the world market price for scrap metal dives significantly below the contracted price.

The Chicago company continues to make monthly shipments in full compliance with the contract. The Chinese continue paying, but are losing $250,000 a month compared to the prevailing open market price. The Chengdu representatives try to get out of the contract or renegotiate, but the Americans won't and don't have to. The Chinese will lose several million dollars over the course of the remaining months on the contract.

Failing to get new terms, the Chinese focus goes internal. It's time to assess blame. Back in Chengdu, management is acutely aware of the shortfall, and sets up an internal meeting to discuss the contract. There are no Americans in on this meeting, because none work for this company. If this were a Chinese company in the U.S., those on lowest point of the hierarchy – the Americans – would almost certainly be blamed.

Three potential scapegoats emerge from the meeting in Chengdu:

1. All the documents were reviewed by the company's Chinese lawyers, and not co-reviewed by a hired American law firm. The Chinese legal counsel could be an easy mark.

2. The contract was also reviewed by company's Economic staff, which was charged with forecasting industry trends and prices. The leader of that unit could be vulnerable, unless he or she is able to push blame down the department's ladder.

3. The Distribution group, charged with communicating with customers about their needs, is also worried.

So, who will take the hit? At subsequent meetings, junior individuals from the three departments are identified and discussed:

1. Legal has a young lawyer, Ms. Bo, who is only familiar with the Chinese legal system. However, this contract was executed under U.S. law.

2. The Economic staff has Mr. Yuan, a mid-level forecaster (Level 3) who was recently criticized for not strictly following company practices – he has been a few minutes late twice in the past month.

3. The Distribution staff recently said goodbye to Mr. Dong, who retired at age 60 (mandatory) just after the contract was signed, and before the first shipment was received.

The matter goes before the Executive Committee of the company, which includes the heads of the three target areas -- but they're all in good standing. The CEO makes it clear that the purpose of the meeting is to understand who (one person) was responsible for the mistake. Each of the executives speaks in turn. None focus on the cause of the error, but only try to deflect blame from their respective departments. On the second round, they offer up Ms. Bo, Mr. Yuan, and Mr. Dong.

After extended discussions (this could go on for hours), the CEO takes the floor and says, "It appears from the discussion that the Executive Committee holds Mr. Dong responsible for our unfortunate losses. Since he has recently retired, a letter will be prepared to inform him of his poor business decision, which will be maintained in his business record."

Mr. Dong, meanwhile, has been enjoying his retirement, but always wondered if a letter might arrive castigating him for the $2 million Yuan (about $300,000 US) which disappeared from company accounts over his tenure. When he reads the letter, slapping his retired hand for an overbid contract, he laughs out loud.

WHO'S TO BLAME LESSONS

Get it? Again, here are a few things to know about "Who's to Blame?" Please remember that our point is certainly not to China-bash. We're just trying to highlight how a different system operates (while acknowledging that we've seen some similar behavior on this side of the Pacific).

1. There will always be someone to blame.

2. Unless someone is totally out of favor, the blame will go the lowest possible level.

3. It's not about understanding what went wrong, it's about who did it.

4. It's not unusual for there to be "secret" meetings to decide who's to blame in advance of an announcement.

5. If you're not Chinese, watch your back (see "Climbing the Ladder").

6. Once blamed, you're guilty. There's no opportunity to defend yourself.

7. Punishment will always have some financial repercussion, ranging from no salary increase or bonus to future dismissal (which could take years).

8. American employees of Chinese-owned companies

are preferred targets of blame. If it leads to dismissal, there is the option of fighting via American employment law, but you rarely if ever win. Without a contract, you're an at-will employee.

9. A paper trail won't necessarily help.

10. Remember that the system has overcome all attempts at change or reform.

SIDEBAR:
The Blame Game in Japan

Have you ever heard the expression: "America has a culture of guilt. Japan has a culture of shame?" Let's switch our focus for a moment to this Asian economic powerhouse (albeit one that has retrenched a bit over the past few years).

Here are a few points we've heard about Japan:

- The importance of hierarchy, especially respect for elders, is firmly embedded. After the World War II defeat, the Japanese monarchy – and its Imperial Family – was left in place. General Douglas MacArthur knew that downgrading the Emperor's position would bring widespread public revolt.

- The traditional culture of Japan was long held to be a good example of one in which shame is the primary agent of social control

- The Japanese preference for taking on personal responsibility for failure, frequently misconstrued by Westerners as insincere, is deeply ingrained in their national psyche.

- A businessperson's reputation, or "face," is of paramount importance.

- A manager's key task is to provide an environment where teams can flourish. When teams fail, it's their manager's fault.

We can't remember a single instance where a Chinese business leader apologized when something hit the fan. As we noted in the preceding chapter, the Chinese cultural preference is to find someone at the lowest possible point on the food chain to take the blame.

What a contrast with Japan, where suicide is the leading cause of death for those under 30. Prime Ministers routinely resign with a deep and very public apology. And, when a large Japanese automaker has problems sufficient to order a major recall in America, its leader apologizes to the United States Congress with the klieg lights at full shine.

We'd love to hear from readers who have done business in Japan, and also from those who work for the significant number of Japanese firms in the States. How pervasive is this "Culture of Shame"? Is it changing or so firmly planted in the Japanese culture that it will withstand any attempts at change (which is our observation of the lasting influence of Chinese cultural traditions on its business class).

Please let us know what you think about Japan, and of course any other Asian countries, on our blog:

Never Try to Drink a Chinese Woman Under the Table
[Plus Other Fun and Practical Tips]
www.nevertrythis.net

THE OFFICE RUMOR MILL:

The Real Information Superhighway

 AVE YOU HEARD?

Isn't that the way all rumors start? Have you heard?

Have you heard that book editors are writing stellar reviews of "Never Try to Drink a Chinese Woman Under the Table," and our sales have already topped the million mark, prompting deep conditional love and affection from our agent and publisher?

Hey, we sure hope so. Not yet, maybe ... but perhaps if you tell all your friends...

And that's the point of this chapter: business with the Chinese is all about knowing your way around rumors – their birth, the way they travel, the way they land. It's one of the things you just have to learn if you're going to succeed.

Oh, let's zip in our usual caveat to avoid China-bashing, ahem, rumors. Rumor mills probably exist in any group business situation. But, as was the case with the drinking of alcohol, it's our observation and experience that the Chinese are simply in a different (and far more sophisticated) league when it comes to the informal office information network.

Here are the highlights we have to offer:

- In the larger Chinese culture, it's our observation that rumors serve a very valuable function – an integral part of what is often described as a "Big Brother Syndrome." Everyone sort of keeps an eye on everyone else. Rumors – from the top down, from the bottom up, from the middle out – help to influence public opinion. This is especially relevant in terms of the emerging middle class. There are now lots of people whose opinions matter (at least in the aggregate).

- It's easy enough to find historical precedent in recent Chinese history: rumor mongering was used during early Communist periods to inflict damage on rivals. More recently, we've seen it in the occasional trials of disgraced public officials. Their typical option for recourse: they countercharge that they've been set up.

- Many Chinese in business work at least two full-time jobs: one of them is personal engagement in their company's rumor mill. Virtually everyone participates.

- "Information networks" certainly sounds like a nicer moniker, and is in fact more accurate: what we're describing here are actually more than rumor mills. In a consensus-based business culture, the networks can disseminate information quickly, and soften the blow of any big changes. People get used to whatever's coming in advance of any public announcement – within a company, within a community, and within the larger culture.

- The networks are often very truthful, filled with snippets of information being fed to people. They grow organically, so that when something is announced, it's part of a chain of information.

- Everyone is a player ... including Westerners at Chinese companies. It's very useful to be able to tap into this information highway. Westerners will typically not become the sort of active players that the Chinese are in terms of starting rumors, but can certainly be part of a rumor's spread.

- Of course, length of service and personal relationships will come into play in terms of how quickly someone will become trusted enough to receive inside information. For Westerners, remember you are outsiders, so extra diligence is essential.

- We gotta say it again: though this may be especially apparent in Asian-owned businesses, it certainly isn't exclusive to them. Water coolers operate everywhere.

- It can get vicious, because rumor mills can also function as revenge networks. Even at a low level, if someone feels they've been treated unfairly, they can start a rumor. We have seen instances where rumors are started about those in upper management (i.e., alleging an executive took his wife to a spa and passed it off as a business trip). Of course, there is some risk to the instigator of a rumor. If it's traced back, there will be consequences.

- Even when a rumor is totally ridiculous – the angry instigator just makes something up – it will be investigated and discussed. And, even if it's eventually understood to be completely false, the very allegation means residual damage for the subject of the rumor. It's sort of like that old adage, "When did you stop beating your wife?"

- You'd think almost every executive would end up tainted, even if by wild-sounding rumors that are eventually revealed to be totally false. But, that doesn't happen, because those who are truly in power have cultivated their own strong networks, which are capable of deflecting rumors – and investigating the sources of scurrilous information.

- Our best advice: be cautious. Especially when you're new, consider what you say and how it will be perceived. Again, Westerners are probably not going to be trusted enough to start a rumor that gets any traction. But, they will certainly be involved in the information network as the tasty tidbits move through an organization. Bottom line: you need to be careful, but probably not as careful as your Chinese colleagues.

- As a new employee in a Chinese-owned company, you'll quickly learn whose rumors turn out to be correct, and whose information can be trusted and safely passed along. Try to stay away from the big stuff – that someone's job is on the line, or a major change is

THE OFFICE RUMOR MILL:

coming. You'll get a sense for scale pretty quickly too.

- Always pay attention to those in power, and what they're doing and saying and who they seem to be favoring.

- Diligence is required not only when dealing with those above you, but certainly also for those at your level – you never know when something will come back to haunt you. And below you too. Who can you trust? It's why people are basically on call all the time – the more involved they are, the less likely they are to miss something. If you're the first to leave the room, people can talk about you, and can decide things when you're not around.

CASE STUDY

Have you ever met someone in business who is so nasty that you wonder why he or she is still employed? Meet Jed, the Western employee of a Chinese company. We were going to call him "Rick," but that would rhyme with the kind of guy he is.

Jed is nominally in charge of new business development, but he's really the western face – or "Big Nose" – of the business. He's just fronting the operation. Most of his employees are young Chinese expats. Jed has achieved notoriety as a supervisor who is more than willing to betray his subordinates whenever something goes amiss.

Here's how it often works: Jed's staff do all the legwork on new business prospects. Jed nominally reviews their work and then bumps it up to a management committee. During the committee meetings, if someone detects a flaw in a proposal, Jed will immediately switch sides, going from the presenter of the proposal to its chief critic – while his hapless employees are stuck in the back of the room, never knowing when he might turn on them.

Ever have a boss like Jed? If so, ever wish you could turn the tables? If you're working in a Chinese-owned company, you have an option.

Caren (the chosen, Americanized name of a young Chinese expat) had the misfortune of working for Jed. Like many of her colleagues, she had forgotten the number of times Jed had been mean to her. His office chatter was filled with racist and sexual innuendo. And then there was the part about getting her painfully-researched new business proposals shot down in management meetings, for reasons that seemed completely arbitrary (like, someone was in a bad mood at the meeting, and needed something to bitch about).

Caren had a good friend in Human Resources, and one day over lunch asked why Jed was able to wield the power he did, the way he did.

"Well, he was hired by a previous general manager, who wanted to give the company more of a Western face," was the reply. Could be a hint that the protection Jed once enjoyed might no longer be present, don't you think?

"Have you heard about the way he treats his staff?" Caren asked.

"We have," was the discreet reply. Actually, Caren's friend in HR had a grudge against Jed. Being in HR, she had access to everyone's salaries. And she knew that Jed was making twice what she was. Ouch!

Now, let's throw in the family angle: Jed does not know that Caren's uncle is a senior executive with the firm at headquarters back in China. When she saw him at a family event, he of course asked her how she was progressing at work (and that's just the way he'd probably ask it ... not the American "how's the job?").

Caren's reply? "I don't know whether the office Big Nose is carrying his weight."

Step back: do you see what Caren has done? She's planted

two seeds in very fertile ground. That's all she has to do. A two-pronged campaign is underway. Jed is on the plate.

Jed's fortunes go into the fire when Caren's friend in HR heads back to China for a meeting to discuss executive performance in the American office. The meeting is convened by – who else – Caren's uncle.

He now takes the lead, and making direct reference to Jed, notes "we've got a problem here."

Meantime, another rumor has started about Jed back at the office (not surprising, given how unpopular and nasty he has been to employees). It starts slowly, but then evolves into a rumor that a new executive is being sent from China, who will be Jed's new direct supervisor – a new layer in between him and the general manager.

What's happening? Step back again: do you know that dynamic of people sitting around in a circle, where one person passes a rumor to the person on their immediate right, and that person passes it on to their immediate right, and on and on around the circle? The story will completely change by the time it makes it around the entire circle, right?

That's what happens here. This piece is totally untrue – there are no plans to bring in a new handler for Jed – but even this inaccurate rumor contributes to the developing consensus that something needs to be done about this man who publicly ridicules his employees. No one will be surprised if "something" happens.

A quick note here: Caren's uncle back in China probably doesn't know about the lower level rumor zipping around the company. Wouldn't care if he did. His sole focus is an unhappy niece, and the knowledge that a Big Nose is causing the problem. The Director of New Business Development has broken the rules by repeatedly treating people badly in a relatively open meeting environment. It's entirely acceptable to treat employees coarsely in private.

Tip: never treat someone badly. You never know who they might be related to.

So, back to the story: the rumor mill's gears keep turning as Jed continues his clueless lurch around the company. Managers are hearing bad things about Jed from trusted colleagues, and are passing it along. Of course, as the "is there a problem?" question travels, so too does speculation as to what the problem might be. Rumors can fill any open space. When people don't know, they guess. There's a rumor that a new executive is on the way top the list, and further that he may be arriving next week! Or is it a "she" who may be setting up shop in two weeks? Either way, the message is essentially the same, and serves the same purpose.

Things continue to cook for a while (the Chinese have all the time in the world), during which Jed acts just as he always does: belligerent, self-centered, and maybe even having a really good quarter: his new business tally is up, which is all the previous general manager ever cared about. Jed thinks all is well.

But then one Friday, Jed's normal 2p.m. presentation is moved to 1p.m. He spends the hour as he typically does: presenting new business proposals, but ready at a moment's notice to throw any of his staff under the bus.

At 2p.m., Jed is called into an impromptu meeting with the head of Human Resources and an HR assistant – a witness. Jed is invited to resign. There's no discussion of his numbers. He's told that the company has decided to restructure. Starting with him.

By the way, the general manager would not attend the meeting. He left the building at 1:58 for another meeting. His hands shall remain clean, and Jed will be escorted out before he returns. Who wants a confrontation?

Jed's departure precipitates a "Ding Dong" party at the office. The Chinese expats have never gone to one, but once the "Wizard of Oz" reference is explained to them by their Western colleagues, they are more than happy to join in for one or two or three or four or five or six drinks.

RUMOR MILL LESSONS

Jed got what he deserved, right? Perhaps he'll be a better human being for it (nah, we doubt that too. He'll probably go on to do the same thing at some other company).

Here are the lessons Jed never learned, that we should all pay attention to when working in an Asian-owned business:

1. The rumor mill is an important fact of professional life, and serious consequences may come to those who do not at least respect its presence and influence.

2. These informal information networks are much more sophisticated and all-inclusive than those found at Western businesses, reflecting the consensus-building nature of the Chinese people.

3. Culture trumps all. Again. Insulting his employees in an open venue was just stupid on Jed's part. It's just not done.

4. Precedent is more than available to explain the prominence of rumor mills. See: "Cultural Revolution, China," wherever good history is sold. You won't have to go far to find current examples either.

5. Though we used the story of Jed to illustrate how the rumor mill can bring someone down, it's just as likely

that the office network will be used to introduce a new idea or soften the blow of impending change.

6. Rumor mills are a vehicle to buck the hierarchy at Chinese businesses. A low-level employee can bring down a senior manager with a well-placed (and well-timed) rumor. Of course, it helps if others would like to see the senior manager knocked off his or her pedestal.

7. Close attention to the information network is just one reason why the Chinese spend so much time on the job – they risk missing something if they're not around.

8. Western employees can expect to invest significant time and effort before they're trusted to join the networks, if they're allowed in at all.

9. Remember that what goes around comes around: if you're invited to play, be careful how you play.

10. Rumor mills aren't only found at Chinese businesses. They're just better at it than Western-owned companies.

SIDEBAR:
Digital Rumor Mills

We focused mostly on person-to-person communication in this chapter. A rumor mill within an Asian-owned company relies on one person talking to another, who talks to another, until the original message moves through the whole company.

But what happens when we enter the digital world, when online rumors can zip around too quickly for censors to block? Back in 2011, false reports circulated that Jiang Zemin had died. In a country that often suppresses the free flow of information, the rumors took on a life of their own – until Zemin appeared in public, quite alive.

So, we couldn't help but wonder: what happens when digital technology collides with a rumor mill? Are there some communications that will only be passed by word of mouth? Or will a disgruntled employee of a Chinese company start tweeting about a despised supervisor? (It begs the question: if someone thinks they can truly remain anonymous online, why wouldn't they apply the rules of information office networks to their online lives, perhaps as separate personas?).

We'd love to hear what you think, both in Chinese-owned businesses, and of course in any relevant experience or observation you have throughout the world of Asian business.

Please post your thoughts on our blog:

Never Try to Drink a Chinese Woman Under the Table

[Plus Other Fun and Practical Tips]
www.nevertrythis.net

PERFORMANCE APPRAISALS:

Better to be an Idiot than 10 Seconds Late

ET'S SAY IT'S 9:02 A.M. at an American company. Will everyone be at their desks? Probably not.

Someone comes in at 9:05, saying "What awful traffic this morning!" Will that person be considered late? Probably not.

Do most American office workers have to punch a time clock on their way into the office each and every morning? Probably not.

Okay, let's switch gears, and you already know which way we're going.

Let's say it's 9:02 at a Chinese-owned American company. Will everyone have clocked in by nine? Yes.

If someone comes in at 9:05 bitching about the traffic, will that person be considered late? Yes.

Do most non-executive office workers at Chinese-owned companies have to punch a time clock? Yes.

If you pride yourself on being really, really punctual, or almost always early, you're going to love working at a Chinese-owned company. If not, you might want to seriously consider working somewhere else.

The Chinese pay serious attention to punctuality. It's one of the more distinctive standards we've found in the performance evaluations issued at their companies in the West.

We're going to dig into the performance appraisal process a bit. Here are the points we'd like to highlight:

- The thought process is very different from a Chinese management structure to a Western one. (Yeah, we know, we've said this a few times already. It bears repeating, especially as we explore the "logic" around how you might be evaluated as an employee in a Chinese-owned company).

- An employee of a Western company will most likely have a comprehensive job description with clear performance objectives and an understanding of how the performance appraisal process works.

- In the Chinese environment, it's rare to have a written job description ... and even more unusual to have performance objectives established. Like to place odds? We'd say that the likelihood of a formal, regular review with your superior is less than 50-50.

- Chinese businesspeople who have grown up in Mainland China understand the rules so it's thought there's no need for anything to be put in writing.

- As a Westerner in a Chinese company, you could go several years without a formal evaluation (if you ever get one).

- Salary adjustments are at the whim of the executive in charge, so there are typically no published salary grades.

- You'll only be frustrated if you use your Western performance experience as a comparison standard with what you should expect or receive. Easier said than done, but still…

- Even if you do receive a written performance evaluation, it will often not be the basis for salary adjustments.

- Those Chinese managers who try to put in place Western structures -- management by objectives, a performance appraisal process, etc. -- will likely fail. Why? Because Western business processes conflict with Chinese cultural imperatives, and culture always trumps. We've seen sincerely-motivated Chinese managers set up elaborate Western-style systems, then completely contradict themselves when it's time to determine where real money will be spent.

- "Better to be an idiot than 10 seconds late," isn't much of an exaggeration. Chinese businesses are fanatical about punctuality. It is typical to require all employees except upper management to punch in.

If an employee is less than even a minute late, it's a serious transgression. A tally of more than a few of these transgressions means kissing a salary increase good bye.

- The emphasis on punctuality means a frantic rush to the clock every morning. Friends will clock in others who are running late – though this is a serious offense if caught. Periodically, you can expect crackdowns.

- If you claim lateness due to transportation failure, you need a note from the relevant transit authority. Just saying there was a lot of traffic won't cut it.

- Clocking in on time doesn't mean you have to immediately start to work. Once you've punched in, you can go get coffee or breakfast. Don't you love that?

- It's irrelevant how long you remain at the office. If work needs to be done, staying late is expected. All that really counts is showing up on time. As for when to leave, a good rule of thumb (at any company, Western or Chinese) is to always leave after your boss.

- Here's our favorite: the Chinese believe it's important to take a nap after lunch. If you have an office, you can just close the door and snooze for half an hour. Those without offices often take power naps at their desks. Seriously!

CASE STUDY

Let's compare and contrast two employees of a Chinese-owned insurance company in the U.S. Both know the rules of the game (it's rigged), but each will experience a very different outcome.

The employer is Quality One Insurance, a Chinese-owned and managed company in the United States. Quality One is focused on consumer-based insurance products like homeowners and renters policies. Quality One has 350 employees, and is heavily weighted towards Chinese management. Expats come to Quality One for a three- to five-year stint before moving on to another Chinese-owned company. Quality One hires American management talent on a limited basis to help minimize regulatory concerns.

John is an experienced U.S. businessman in his early 50's. Though not an executive, he is a well-respected senior manager. John has spent the majority of his career at other insurance companies, but he's been with Quality One for more than 10 years. He specializes in consumer compliance. In his years with the company, John quickly came to understand the structure of the organization, and works diligently to strengthen the compliance environment – with a particular emphasis on satisfying government regulators.

As the compliance field mushroomed, John's department grew. Ninety percent of his staff are entry level, mostly young Chinese expats with no prior experience. John has mentored many future business leaders for Quality One.

As for his personal professional habits, John is text book: an early arrival at work, always at his desk by 7:45a.m. He rarely leaves before 7:30 at night. Unlike his Chinese counterparts, he works non-stop, doesn't do business lunches, and doesn't have time for the typical after-lunch nap.

By every typical measure, John is a particularly effective spokesman for the company. He has frequent visits from government officials, including those from the District Attorney's office, and insurance regulators concerned with potential money laundering. He has established an outstanding relationship with these officials, winning their respect to such an extent that they will often seek his counsel on non-Quality One business practices.

It's time for John's performance appraisal. He's called in by his superior, the Chinese general manager now in his second year at Quality One. John is given a formal document, with numerical grades filled out for individual tasks and objectives. There are no written comments, just the grades.

John reviews his evaluation on the one-to-five scale (one is unacceptable; five is exceptional). Under prior management, John got 4's and 5's -- recognized as the company star that his government regulators know him to be.

But this year, his second with a new manager, he gets mostly 3's. The only oral feedback: "You have too many people in your department." John suppresses a laugh and a desire to roll his eyes. His staffing level is mandated by the government regulators.

In the bigger picture, John is taken aback, justifiably angry, and disappointed. He knows how hard he works, and how many problems he has helped Quality One avoid. But, as we said, John has been around this company for 10 years. He was prized by the last Chinese general manager. The current guy ... not so much. Understanding how the system works, John remains silent, signs the evaluation, and leaves the office. When salary increases and bonuses are distributed, John gets only a token nod.

He has two options: eat it, or leave. John has no appetite for a job search well into his 50's, and decides to lay low and suffer in silence. Maybe a new general manager will come along.

Can you guess what's going to happen with the other guy? We hope so ... that means you're learning from this book. Let's go through it:

Chen Haiying has been in United States for two years, coinciding with the tenure of Quality One's current general manager. Haiying is not in the same league as John when it comes to relevant business expertise, but is totally expert in massaging egos, and is always present at the right time to open a door, pour a cup of tea, or provide any other service. He has an unyielding approach to his employees: ordering them about, offering no flexibility, and creating what most HR types would call a hostile work environment.

Haiying has been successful in hiring a key group of subordinates who are industry experts and cover his own personal lack of experience. He sees himself akin to foreign ambassadors, who get their positions based on who they know (or have raised money for), surrounding themselves with those who know the substance. Haiying is hungry to move up the ladder, and understands that his relationship with the general manager is key. Whenever a delegation of Chinese officials visit, Haiying is front and center: organizer, hand shaker, car door opener, whatever. Over two years with the company, he's been given more and more responsibility, resulting in more and more staff. Haiying believes he always knows more and better than others, regardless of his true abilities.

Fast-forward to Haiying's performance appraisal. He goes to the general manager's office and is given a reception quite unlike the one John experienced. He's immediately given a cup of tea, enjoys an informal chat with his boss, and then is told he's doing an outstanding job. The numerical grades are mostly 5's. When the money comes, Haiying gets among the largest salary increases and bonuses in the company. His future, at least under this general manager, is assured.

BETTER TO BE AN IDIOT LESSONS

Not too surprising, right?   As we've said over and over, personal relationships and deference often count a whole lot more among the Chinese than simple competence.   What John did worked under the first general manager, but he made a big mistake assuming his methods would work with the second.

Here's our list of lessons, and you'll note some are more applicable to entry- and mid-level employees that those who enjoy the perks of upper management:

1. Never be late (unless you're a senior employee ... then just say you were out at a meeting).

2. Understand that your experience in a Chinese company will be very different than at a Western company.

3. Don't expect a formal performance appraisal.

4. Don't expect a comprehensive job description.

5. Don't expect clearly defined objectives for your job.

6. Don't be surprised if you have to punch a time clock, especially if you're just starting out in your career.

7. Understand there is a separate and distinct evaluation and reward process for your Chinese colleagues. It's

not necessarily easier for them, but it's different. Lots of Chinese workers don't enjoy the glad-handing and tea-pouring that seem so necessary to success. But they do it.

8. Play defense: if you're making a lateral move from another company into a Chinese company, make sure you get the most attractive package you can going in, with written guarantees, before you start. You may end up with a general manager, like John did, who just doesn't see your value.

9. If you don't have a sense of humor about this entire process, go someplace else to work.

10. An appreciation of irony helps too.

SIDEBAR:

Are We On Time?

We admit it: the Chinese business fixation with punctuality cracks us up, especially the part where you can't show up one minute late, but you can go get breakfast once you clock in – and take a nap after lunch.

So, as is our habit with these sidebars, let's try to broaden out the experience a bit. Usually we just think about the other countries in Asia, but on this topic we need to cast an even wider net: punctuality didn't start with the Chinese. Have you ever taken a train in Switzerland or many other European capitals? They are militantly on time!

We're fascinated by the sociological research indicating punctuality is one of the standards by which international business cultures can be judged, meaning that the more developed the business culture is in an individual country, the more it will prize punctuality in a business setting.

And we're also familiar with the great distinctions in the importance of the clock that seem to come within cultures, notably between generations. We think always showing up late is a great way for kids to goad their business-oriented parents. Check out the traffic online: there are blogs filled with Asian kids complaining when someone is late; and also taking umbrage when a romantic prospect shows up early!

We'd love to hear from readers about their experiences.

Have you ever been 30 seconds late at a Chinese-owned company? How about anywhere else in Asia: how much do people care about time? Is the time fixation just a business culture thing, or does it generalize across cultures? Is time a tool for children to rebel against their executive parents?

Please let us know what you think on our blog:

Never Try to Drink a Chinese Woman Under the Table
[Plus Other Fun and Practical Tips]
www.nevertrythis.net

WHEN DOES "YES"

Actually Mean Yes?

MOST DICTIONARIES DEFINE "yes" pretty simply: an adverb used to express affirmation or assent.

But, the Chinese Business Dictionary (if one existed), would have a much more layered, much less precise definition. Among the Chinese doing business, sometimes "yes" means yes. Sometimes it doesn't. We can offer some signals and clues as to which is which under differing circumstances. Here are the points we'd like to highlight:

- As with most things with the Chinese, inside culture trumps all. You are an outsider.

- In the West, one person may have the authority (after due diligence) to authorize a deal. Not so with the Chinese: one person may make the announcement, but it always represents a unanimous group. See the lessons from our "Art of Consensus" chapter. The Chinese decision model relies on consensus.

- In China, you'll never hear a "yes" that means anything on your first meeting, unless you have something to offer that the Chinese need now and cannot find anywhere else.

- You can be easily misled by positive feedback. The Chinese may say "yes" to make you feel good, and help you to avoid loss of face.

- It is very difficult to read the subtle signals that the Chinese will pass between themselves.

- Just because you get some level of affirmation (like smiles and nodding heads), don't fool yourself into believing that you're doing a great job or have a deal.

- The number of Chinese who show up for a meeting will be an important signal as to your relative importance: in general, the more the better. If 12 people show up for a meeting, and they're mostly executives, you're golden. The big exception is if you already have long-established relationships – then the number in the room doesn't matter as much.

- If you have a meeting scheduled with a Chinese executive, and someone else appears in his or her place, it probably means that you've been judged to be not important at that time. Hang on; that could change.

- The Chinese have a different sense of time than Westerners do. It's sort of meaningless to them. You could have three, four or five meetings that come to nothing. Don't think multiple meetings mean you have a working relationship.

- If the Chinese call you for a meeting, it probably means a sincere interest on their part.

- They will usually assent to your request for a meeting, but don't take that as positive reinforcement that they want whatever you've got. They're just being gracious as their culture dictates.

- Getting to an agreement: more often than not, it won't happen in an office. It'll happen over shared food in a restaurant.

CASE STUDY

We ended our highlights with a restaurant reference for a reason: it's a great way to segue to our case study with an old friend.

Remember Tom, the grain salesman from Indiana we met in our chapter on food? He's back! Tom not only survived his first trip to China and his first banquet meal, but he's still in the running for a significant amount of business. Let's see whether he's able to land it.

Our first observation about Tom is that he shouldn't feel special. Getting a warm initial reception in China, as well as an introductory banquet, is pretty routine. The big question is whether Tom gets past the first trip.

On Tom's initial visit, he had meetings all day long with four Chinese executives. The meetings were held as a group. In addition to the four executives, there were three other Chinese participants who were busy taking notes, filling teacups, and answering text messages on their phones.

Tom was a little confused, because the meeting style was so different from what he was used to. Tom had prepared a Power Point presentation to facilitate a discussion about the capabilities of Indiana Grain and the advantages it would bring to the Chinese company. As he began the presentation, he encouraged the executives to interrupt him with questions at any point. As his presentation continues, Tom notices that one of the executives had fallen asleep, and no one was asking any questions. He wondered whether or not they really understood English, but of course he couldn't ask that. When he completed his presentation, he again asked if there were any questions, and was met with a resounding silence.

Following his presentation and the meeting, he was given a tour of the Chinese company's offices, and then was treated to the sumptuous banquet we described a while ago with all the bizarre food.

A few points about Tom's first meeting: it was important that he met all four executives together. It indicated significantly more interest than if he had separate meetings. Also, he shouldn't put too much stock in positive affirmations (a smile, a head nod), from any one individual. At the same time, he shouldn't read anything into the fact that one of them fell asleep – that's a culturally acceptable practice at a Chinese business.

It would be unrealistic for Tom to expect a decision on any sort of deal on his first visit – but of course Tom didn't know that, because his American experience sometimes did yield immediate results. As we've said, the only thing that would motivate a quick response would be if something happened that made his grain an immediate must-have. We mean something big, like a pending famine, or inside information that the world commodity price is about to jump. On this first visit, the Chinese would be most interested in making Tom's acquaintance. They wouldn't care that he flew around the globe to meet them.

Same rules apply to Tom's first banquet. It's a reflection of Chinese culture to treat newcomers very graciously. It doesn't necessarily mean they'll want to do business, and almost certainly won't want to enter into any deals right away. Tom is a virgin in terms of doing business with the Chinese, and he doesn't know what the signs may or may not mean ... so he returns to Indiana, and reports to his boss that a deal would be quickly signed.

But then time starts to drag. Over the course of the next four months, Tom stays in ongoing contact by email with his Chinese counterparts, but he makes little progress in moving the deal forward. He starts to question whether he'll ever see China again.

Then, to his surprise, Tom opens his email one morning: an invitation to return to China for further meetings. He boards a plane and flies around the world with renewed optimism, but this second meeting is almost a mirror image of the first. Tom notices that there are a few more executives and a few more tea-pourers at his all-day session, and sees some vigorous head nodding. Our man from Indiana, a true salesman at heart, now feels certain that a deal is at hand, and he can return home with his reputation secured as an international businessman.

But again, the clock is not with Tom. A few more months pass, with no real encouragement that a deal is in the works. Can you imagine how frustrating that would be?

Next step in our scenario: the Chinese accept Tom's invitation to send a delegation to Indiana. They ask for a full-day program for their executives to visit Indiana Grain's facilities and a farm which supplies the company.

Throw in a surprise: the Chinese inform Tom that the delegation will include a senior official from the Chinese

Ministry of Agriculture, as well as several officials from the Ministry of Chinese Trade. When Tom sees the list of add-ons, he doesn't know what to make of it.

What Tom should have known (too bad he didn't read our book), was that bringing along a government delegation is typically a red flag that not much is going to happen. It means the trip's main purpose is not to do business. It's an exploratory trip that may have several goals, but probably won't include contract negotiations. Further, since the delegation will be flying through Chicago, it probably means that they plan to go shopping.

Tom knows enough not to attempt a Chinese banquet in Indianapolis. Midwestern-style Kung Pao Chicken would not be a hit. Instead, he hosts a barbeque for the visiting delegation. The visitors are extremely gracious and try all of the various charred foods placed before them. They don't eat all of them, but everyone loves one of the barbeque's offerings: the on-tap beer!

Once again, Tom is heartened. As the beer flows, the number and sincerity of the toasts seems to increase. A deal must finally be at hand, right?

Well, no. The delegation headed to Chicago for some high-end shopping, and Tom had his hands full trying to justify the cost of the barbeque to his boss.

Two months (yep, another two months) pass, with several gracious emails but no encouragement that a contract can be executed.

Then, Tom gets a phone call from China. Not an email, and

take special note because this is important, but a personal phone call, asking Tom if he can return to China the following week.

Tom's boss wants to cut his losses, and bail on this Chinese prospect. Tom begs to go, just this one last time, because if something did come through Indiana Grain could be in an entirely different business climate. And Tom would be a star.

Tom doesn't know the motivation for the telephone call. We'll tell you: the Chinese had learned of a pending crop failure in one of the Southern provinces. State-controlled media had not reported it, and are doing their best to hold off international reporting on behalf of companies like Tom's Chinese counterparts. Yes, this sort of thing really happens.

Truth be told, Tom is facing his own internal conflict on his Chinese prospect. People are laughing at him at Indiana Grain. A barbeque for a Chinese delegation who did nothing but drink, toast, and then go shopping in Chicago? And, the excitement of going to China has definitely worn off. Once you experience all that jet lag over the course of several trips, it can really wear you down.

"One more time. If nothing happens, again, we bag it." That's the agreement between Tom and his boss. Off he goes.

This time, Tom does not get any immediate signals that the climate had changed. About the same number of people show up at the meeting. But here's the critical difference: this time, one of the Chinese executives takes the lead and is more focused on moving discussions forward.

And then, viola! Tom is invited to a second banquet. He is

seated next to the chairman of the company, whom he's never met.

During the first toast, the Chairman stands up and says: "We look forward to a long and mutually beneficial relationship. Contracts will be exchanged next week. We will expect the first shipment shortly thereafter."

Tom almost falls out of his chair. A star is born.

WHEN DOES YES ACTUALLY MEAN YES LESSONS

Here's our list of lessons for you to sense when "yes" actually, really and truthfully does mean yes:

1. On your first encounter with a Chinese business, don't be fooled by positive affirmations like smiles, or head nods, or even the word "yes" uttered by someone in the room in answer to a question. The Chinese are gracious people. They want you to feel good.

2. If you encounter a large group at a meeting, it's generally an indication of positive interest.

3. If you end up meeting with a very small group, or if substitutes appear, it generally indicates a lack of interest at that time.

4. Don't be thrown if participants in a meeting fall asleep. It's culturally acceptable for them to do so, and is no indication of interest or lack of it.

5. Don't expect to cut a deal in a single meeting, unless you have something the Chinese desperately need. You are working in their time frame, which is to say time and the number of meetings don't really matter.

6. Within the Chinese business context, decisions will not be made in front of you. They aren't hashed out in a meeting with Westerners. Decisions are the product of group consensus, usually arrived at privately.

7. Remember that meetings are important, but not as important as meals for building trust with potential Chinese business partners. Restaurants easily trump offices.

8. It's fairly routine for new business contacts to have a banquet hosted in their honor.

9. It's relatively special for new business contacts to have a second banquet hosted in their honor. It may mean a working relationship and deals are imminent.

10. You now have extra reasons to know your way around a Chinese banquet (i.e., eating bizarre food that is served to you, and drinking challenges).

SIDEBAR:

Does "Yes" Mean Yes Anywhere in Asia?

Asian cultures in general are known for their courtesy and graciousness. They're also known for not necessarily saying what they mean.

So, what does "yes" mean across Asian cultures? We've been dealing mostly with China, but here are some observations that we've heard from multiple sources:

- "Yes" may simply mean "I have heard what you said," rather any sort of affirmative answer, in many Asian countries.

- Saying "no" is a difficult thing for many Asians to do, especially on a personal level. If they say "no," even if they mean it, they may be setting up a situation where someone will lose face.

- Often the word "difficult" is used instead of "no."

- Asians often find it more polite to say, "I'm sorry, but I don't think I will be able to ...," instead of saying "no."

- In India, a very loose wobble of the neck from side to side – the Indian Wiggle – can mean yes, no, or anything in between. When accompanied by a sound, like a "hunh," then it's more likely to mean "yes."

- Okay, this isn't Asia, but we have to include it: Bulgarians nod their heads to say "no" and shake them to say "yes." In Britain, "possibly" often means "no." In France, "no" usually means "no," and is often accompanied by a frown. Aren't cultural traditions fascinating?

So, as is our habit, let's turn it over to you: we'd love to hear from readers about their experiences. Have you ever received nothing but positive affirmations in Asia, but then had the prospective business fall through? When do Asians – especially in business settings – say "yes" and mean it? Are there other lessons here for the rest of us?

Please let us know what you think on our blog:

Never Try to Drink a Chinese Woman Under the Table [Plus Other Fun and Practical Tips] www.nevertrythis.net

NEVER TRY TO DRINK A CHINESE WOMAN UNDER THE TABLE

FOCUS

Just Give Us What We Want!

E KICKED AROUND SOME alternate titles for the last chapter and this one. Instead of "When Does 'Yes' Actually Mean Yes?" we could have gone with "Doing Business With the Chinese." This chapter could be named "Doing Business For the Chinese (As an Employee)." But those were kind of boring, and as you know we have short attention spans. So, instead, let's talk about Focus. Who knows where we'll end up?

Here are the highlights of this chapter. We apologize in advance, because some of them are a little depressing, and indicate we live in a very imperfect world:

- Colonialism may be on the wane as a governing principle among nations, but it is alive and well in international business. When you are the employee of a Chinese-owned business, you are treated quite like a loyal subject of the Empire: "just do as we say, and don't ask questions."

- "Business Colonialism" certainly isn't exclusive to the Chinese. In our experience, if you're a Western employee of a foreign-owned enterprise, the home office always (thinks it) knows best. Same thing for American companies operating all over the world, who take their marching orders from New York or Chicago or Los Angeles.

- In our experience and observation, Chinese companies in the West are always managed by headquarters back in China. Profit targets are set by the home office without regard to local conditions, and lines of business and new product development are controlled and mandated from Guangzhou or Beijing or Shanghai.

- Unrealistic expectations are the rule, since the Chinese in China often assume they can duplicate whatever works there in another country. Not so far off from what the British did in India, is it?

- Again, with the caveat that this is based on our observation and there are certainly exceptions to be found, the Chinese and their businesses in the West are duplicators, not creators. Theirs is not an inventive, entrepreneurial business culture. Their historical strength has been their ability to be the low-cost provider, and that's the way they think.

- Authority emanates from whatever level of the hierarchy is above you, and can be very autocratic. The Chinese do not necessarily treat their American employees with lots of cultural understanding. They often just say, "Here's what we want you to do. No questions. Just do it." And they aren't selling sneakers. Except when they are.

- Again, just so we don't look as though we're China-bashing: When you work for a foreign corporation in your country, you can reasonably expect them to adopt a "we know best" attitude. You need to be okay with that, or your job will be a miserable way to pay your bills.

- It's very common for the Chinese to put in very long days. Really, 16 hours a day happens all the time. But that doesn't mean they're always working. Post-lunch naps, falling asleep in meetings, and long hours of drinking and dining with customers all count. On top of that, part of the day can include secret Communist Party meetings for political education.

- As a Westerner, you will probably not be expected to match your Chinese colleagues in hours on the job. In fact, they probably won't want you to. You most likely will not be included in the social outings, and they won't want you to have too much inside information. You're an outsider, a hired hand.

- It is very typical for a Chinese business in America, operating at the behest of the home office back home, to embark on new projects in a fairly arrogant (and sometimes kind of clueless) fashion, ignoring local cultural imperatives and even immovable business constraints – like government regulations. There's no real planning or attention paid to due diligence and competitive analysis.

- Within a Chinese-operated business, your boss knows what's best for you. And her boss knows what's best for her. And her boss' boss. And her boss' boss' boss. You get the idea. Everyone has a boss.

CASE STUDY

Meet Phil, our latest ambitious, hardworking, and experienced Western businessman about to learn the different reality of Chinese business culture.

Phil needed a job after being packaged out of the financial services firm where he worked for 10 years. He wasn't going to ask a lot of questions during the interview process, instead focusing on his rich store of experience and the value he would bring to any new employer.

Golden Dragon Investment Services does a lot of business out of its American headquarters in New York City's Chinatown, and Phil goes through all the motions of the job interview process there: interviews, offer, minimal if any salary negotiation, and acceptance.

All through the drill, Phil is told that his first big project will be to open an office in New York City's "new" Chinatown – Flushing, New York – just a subway ride away from Manhattan. Hallelujah! Phil has a great new job, a hefty paycheck, a big project, and a professional reason to live.

But then the job starts, and Phil quickly comes to learn that his new job is different from what he was led to believe. Uh, oh....

The home office back in Beijing wants the branch in Flushing. Because of regulatory restrictions, Golden Dragon is limited to just one office in the New York Metropolitan Area. They're willing to transfer the license currently devoted to the Chinatown operation to the new branch to satisfy American regulators. But, beyond this needed nod to the governmental climate, Phil is shocked to learn that there has been no intelligence-gathering on the prospective new site: no competitive analysis of the services already provided there by competitors, no in-depth market analysis, no assessment of whether technological standards can be met, no hiring of outside counsel, no nothing. Golden Dragon is moving from its long-established office in Chinatown to Flushing because that's what Beijing wants.

Fast forward to the first general management meeting, where Phil wants to make a good impression and point out the obvious holes in the planned move. He can be the savior of the company!

Put on your seatbelt, Phil. Our readers can guess the kind of ride ahead of you.

After the general manager makes a broad pronouncement with no real content, and then asks for questions, Phil details all the preliminary work that should be done before a move is even considered. Everyone in the room listens attentively. Then, the general manager thanks Phil, and moves on to the next agenda item without any discussion of Phil's points – effectively both ignoring and dismissing him. Further, the GM notes that the time frame for the move is six months, so that an executive from China can do the ribbon-cutting during an already-planned trip. Finally, he notes the membership on a special task force to manage the move. Phil isn't on it.

Imagine poor Phil sitting in that meeting. It's a shocking way to learn what is – and what is not – expected of him.

Let's take a step back. It won't surprise you to learn that Phil was hired largely based on his previous experience managing significant projects for New York financial services companies. His presence is intended to soothe American regulators. He's not really going to be trusted with a leadership role on this major endeavor. Or on any other project. He wasn't hired to be a leader. He was hired as an American face. A Big Nose.

Phil believes he has a relatively secure job. But we'd say that all he's got are empty promises about the job he thought he was hired to do. Phil begins to understand just how differently business runs under the direction of a foreign culture.

How does Phil respond? Well, at this point, what can he do? He attends lots of meetings. He tries to build relationships with his new colleagues. He tries to figure out what the hell is going on, and what's going to happen next.

The move lurches forward, guided by Chinese managers more motivated to please their bosses than anything else. It doesn't add up, and the project is plagued by delays.

Golden Dragon does end up hiring outside counsel, and receives regulatory approval to move its New York office from Chinatown to Flushing. Because of the way the project is managed, there are unanticipated expense overruns, and the company is forced to renew its Chinatown lease for two years (there's no way they can move in time – and this added expense adds more than a million dollars to the project's cost).

The general manager remains strategically aloof from all the project's significant milestones – he's trying to make sure that any real or perceived failures aren't his responsibility.

This could end badly, and from other chapters you know that a business failure would likely be blamed on one individual, as low in the hierarchy as possible. It could well be Phil. In fact, who would be better? Brand new at the company, brought in to manage this project, unfortunately ends up being unequal to the task. Maybe Phil's new job isn't so secure after all.

Jump with us into a time machine, and fast forward two years. After repeated and expensive delays, Golden Dragon Investment Services is set to move from Chinatown to Flushing. Just 15 months late!

What happens now? There's a gala ribbon cutting celebration in Flushing, and a lot of upset customers in Chinatown who have no intention of hopping on a subway to follow Golden Dragon.

Following the Grand Opening, the new office is virtually deserted all day long. A few people do wander in, inquire about the range of services, and leave without establishing accounts because the guys across the street offer more for less. None of the anticipated revenue and profit targets are achievable, and the Flushing office loses money rather than adding to the bottom line.

But wait ... let's see what happened to the general manager and Phil. Just prior to the move, the GM got a big promotion and transferred back to Beijing. He's free and clear, and now able to assign blame rather than receive it. His obvious target: our man Phil.

But wait, Phil is no idiot, and all the project delays gave him a chance to contact recruiters with the benefit of being employed. A great job offer comes through – from one of the guys across the street in Flushing!

The GM ends up blaming a junior employee in Legal for the whole Flushing Debacle.

NEVER TRY TO DRINK A CHINESE WOMAN UNDER THE TABLE

FOCUS LESSONS

Here's our list of lessons for you to maintain your focus as the Western employee of a Chinese-owned company:

1. Chinese business is top down. Your role as an employee is "bottoms up." Remember what you were hired for. You have a role to play.

2. People naturally go with what they know. When it comes to a foreign-owned business, the culture of the owner prevails. You're going to find the same thing around the world.

3. In a Chinese-owned business, you're not likely to get a lot of credit for independent thought and initiative. It's all about the team effort. You're more likely to get very specific instructions on tasks to be completed. Individual effort is criticized, not applauded.

4. You'll be spending a lot of your waking hours on the job at a Chinese-owned business. You will be paid near the going market rate for your services.

5. Chinese businesses in the West have to deal with lots of autocratic directives from headquarters, which typically include very unrealistic expectations on the local business climate. There is no room for discussion. Project schedules are typically unrealistically short.

6. Remember what you learned earlier: your job is not necessarily what you are led to believe in the

job interview process. Don't put a lot of stock in job descriptions. Try to be realistic about why you were hired. You won't be able to find skeletons in the closet, but there's a underlying rationale (agreed upon by a group, or forced by regulators) for bringing you aboard.

7. Relationships are crucial within a Chinese company. Of course, pay attention to your boss, but also look for cues from successful colleagues.

8. If you have a need to raise objections or point out flaws in plans, do your best to find a private way to do so. Office relationships are crucial, and you should always get support for any initiative before you walk into a meeting. The "decisions" made in meetings are usually unanimous.

9. Many times, your best approach will be to simply roll with it, and find a way to be okay with whichever way the wind is blowing.

10. Don't discount the value of sheer blind luck. Remember the general manager. Pity the poor junior employee in Legal.

SIDEBAR:

Getting Started in a New Gig

We thought it would be fun to go through a quick tour of the advice typically given to new employees, and compare what would work in an American (or other Western) company versus what would fly in an Asian-owned company.

Some advice is sound, across the board:

- Dress appropriately for the new job: you probably saw a number of people while securing the position; dress like they do.

- Do as much research as you can on your new employer.

- Display a positive, can-do attitude.

- Be ready to follow the office guidelines concerning working hours.

- Build relationships with co-workers.

- Manage your career: keep up with what's going on outside the office in your industry. You never know...

Now, here's some advice commonly given to new employees at American companies that would require significant re-tuning if you want to be successful at an Asian-owned American company:

- "Stand out by showing great individual initiative." Ugh.

Individual success is often a negative. Being singled out for exceptional work can be the kiss of death – it makes you a target. Remember, Asian cultures tend to focus more on groups than they do on individuals. Better to stand out by blending in. Be a team player.

- "Ask managers for meetings to discuss goals and objectives." This one might be okay, but remember that sometimes less is more. In an Asian-owned company, you don't want to come off as too assertive. You want to come off as someone everyone likes and gets along with. Goals and objectives are often less than direct, and may not be measured in regular performance evaluations.

- "Set out to exceed expectations. Show you can deliver." Ah, we do love our friends in Human Resources. Who else could come up with this stuff? Our advice is to be strategic, and always keep in mind that you are an outsider to the predominant business culture of your new employer. Spend your time trying to figure out how it works, and what your optimal role is (it's likely to be different than what you'll get on a job description).

- "Go for early wins and document your successes." Um, no.

- "Learn who's who." Yup, yup, yup. And remember, there's a hierarchy of Asians above you on the food chain.

Of course, our expertise is mostly China, but we've heard

enough from others working for Asian-owned companies that we feel comfortable making these generalizations.

What does your experience tell you? We always like to hear exceptions to the rules. If anything will increase your odds of success when dealing with the various Asian cultures, we want to know about it:

Please let us know what you think on our blog:

Never Try to Drink a Chinese Woman Under the Table [Plus Other Fun and Practical Tips] www.nevertrythis.net

PUTTING IT TOGETHER

OVER THE COURSE OF THIS BOOK, we've tried to throw you into a different world. The Chinese have a distinct culture with unique expectations – probably a sharp contrast to what you learned about Western and American business.

As we say all the time, the Chinese business culture is not better or worse than America's. It's just different, and smart American businesspeople should know what they're dealing with, before they run the risk of offending a business colleague.

Each chapter ended with a list of lessons we want you to learn. To condense them even more, here's an overview of what we consider to be the most important of those lessons:

BLENDING IN:
What to Expect OUTSIDE the Office

FOOD

Food is an extremely important part of the Chinese culture, and you cannot close a deal without building trust over food. For those with tender palates: if you're not open to developing an adventurous sense of dining, it's going to be difficult to do business with the Chinese.

Here's a simple way to figure out where you stand, and to prepare yourself in advance of initial contact with Chinese colleagues: go out to eat at the most authentic Chinese restaurant you can find in your hometown. Let the wait staff know about your sincere interest in Chinese culture, and put yourself in their hands. Say you want to eat what they eat. Failing that, order the strangest-sounding items on the menu, as far afield from your comfort zone as you can go.

Pay as much attention to how this experience feels as to how the food looks and tastes. Are you open to trying new things? Can you at least taste something that looks different than anything you've ever eaten before? You don't have to become an expert in Chinese cuisine, but you will get major points for trying. So, try.

ALCOHOL

In Chinese business culture, alcohol helps to bring down barriers. An evening of shared drinking leads to trust. During a meal, never pick up your wine glass unless you're being toasted or offering a toast. You don't have to go as far as your Chinese colleagues, but (similar to the situation with food) you'll get points for trying. Again, try (unless you have personal reasons for begging off ... if so, be prepared to consistently say that you're on medication that doesn't permit the drinking of alcohol).

SEX

Keep your underwear on – that's pretty good advice for handling the topic of sex in business. But, we're not prudes and we know things happen with people who spent the better part of each workday (and many weekends) together. Still, the power relationships at the office can make for very messy sexual politics, and modern China is very much a mix of current thinking and centuries-old traditions.

So we're gonna say it again: keep your underwear on.

YOUR CHINESE COLLEAGUES:
How They Think, Why They Keep to Themselves, How That's Changing

GENERATIONAL CHANGE

There's no "one size fits all" when it comes to working with the Chinese. There are distinct groups of people with different worldviews, reflecting their experience, based on their age. Your expectations and behavior in business settings should be informed by the age-associated cultural influences on your Chinese counterparts.

NAME BRAND STATUS

Shopping is more than recreation for the Chinese. It's, ahem, serious business. If you're giving a gift to a Chinese business colleague, make sure it's a name brand item – an expensive, prestigious name brand item. Save the goofy ties and cheap pen sets for your American friends.

LOSS OF FACE

The absolute worst transgression you can make around Asians in general and the Chinese in particular is to humiliate someone in public – or to be perceived as having done so. Try to think through your strategies and actions with an eye towards avoiding this faux pas at all costs. Remember that when someone really loses face in a Chinese business context, it's usually part of a very carefully constructed strategy to take someone down.

BIG NOSE

If you are the Western face of a Chinese-owned business, no matter the actual size of your proboscis, you are a Big Nose. At the senior level, Big Noses are often handsomely rewarded with title and salary, but are essentially on-call ambassadors to the local population with no real decision-making power.

LANGUAGE

Chinese business people who apply for overseas postings have to demonstrate English language proficiency before they come abroad. For a Westerner working for a Chinese-owned business, it's a more complicated matter. There's generally no requirement of proficiency in Mandarin or Cantonese – in fact, most Chinese think you can't really know their language unless you grow up with it. Westerners working with the Chinese can learn the language if they want to dedicate themselves to it (it's a very difficult thing to do), and then decide whether they want anyone to know they know. They'll probably overhear a lot more pertinent information if no one in the room thinks they can translate.

FEAR OF FLIGHT

Westerners can take their freedom to travel for granted: time and money willing, they're good to go. Not the case for the Chinese. When they arrive for a foreign posting in the West, their passports are collected at the airport by a specially-designated holder. They get them back when they head home.

The Chinese form a fairly tight-knit community in foreign business capitals, and their country's fear of flight tends to keep them that way.

GOING SOLO VS. GROUP THINK

A life-long emphasis on individual achievement and

recognition is a very Western concept. The Chinese model is focused on group consensus. It's an easy thing to mess up if you're a Westerner going to work for a Chinese-owned company. Don't go looking for a brainstorming session, because you won't find any.

THE CORPORATE ENVIRONMENT:
What to Expect INSIDE the Office

CLIMBING THE LADDER

Organizational charts are fairly standard among Western businesses, but if they exist at a Chinese company, it's probably to make a Western government regulator happy. There are many unwritten rules in a Chinese company, reflecting the way the larger Chinese culture operates. The best way to navigate it is to build relationships with individual colleagues over time.

WHO'S TO BLAME

There WILL always be someone to blame when something goes wrong. It's not about understanding what went wrong, it's about who did it. Blame will accrue to the lowest possible person in the relevant office hierarchy. Try to make sure it isn't you.

RUMOR MILLS

It can be very, very confusing to gauge your level of support for any initiative. So, you need to pay attention to information wherever you can find it.   The rumor mills in Chinese companies are much better developed than in Western ones – and they're usually correct.   The office gossip may be a power broker you need to cultivate.

PERFORMANCE APPRAISALS

A Western Human Resources professional could have a complete meltdown if he or she tried to apply his standards and perceptions to a Chinese company.   Employees typically don't have job descriptions.   You typically will not find a comprehensible salary scale. Raises and bonuses can happen by whim. But one thing's for sure: at anything below the most senior level, no one is ever late. They may clock in and then go to breakfast, but no one is ever late.

WHEN DOES "YES" ACTUALLY MEAN YES?

The Chinese are very gracious people, and want you to feel good. They will offer positive affirmations all the time, which you may mistake as approval for one of your ideas. Never mistake a head nod for an actual "yes."

FOCUS

Just Give Us What We Want!

Like citizens of any other country, Chinese doing business abroad tend to adopt a "we know best" attitude at their owned businesses. Beyond that, and again like many others, the home office back in the native country usually sets the tone and issues the orders. Best to know that going in, and figure out whether you can be okay with it.

FINAL THOUGHTS...

Got it all? Here's our bottom line: Get over yourself and everything you thought you knew from business school or your own experience. Have fun, take advantage of the opportunity to meet new people, try new food, and make the world a slightly smaller place.

At the same time, don't kid yourself that you will be an agent of change in the Chinese corporate culture. You have to play the ball as it is on the field right now. Just learn where and how it falls.

BONUS

Your Maiden Voyage to China

E COULDN'T END THIS book without our thoughts on traveling to China. Some of this information is supplied in bits and pieces in previous chapters, but here's an expanded overview intended to get you through your first trip to China in style!

ADVANCE PLANNING

- To go to China, you'll need a visa. The form is available from the Chinese Consulate online, and there are several different types – tourist and business, single entry and multi entry.

- Most countries in Asia, including China, require your passport have at least six months of valid time remaining before expiration. Make sure you have sufficient pad time on your passport or you won't be allowed in.

- For a trip to China, the easiest to obtain is a single entry tourist visa.

- If you're going to China on business, and apply for a business visa, the bureaucracy will engage and you will need – among other things – a letter of invitation from a Chinese business.

- Many if not most people will apply for a tourist visa even if they're going to China for a business purpose. Richard always did it this way, over the course of more than a decade, and was never questioned.

- A visa to China does not grant entry into Tibet, which the Chinese consider to be part of their country. A special travel document required for Tibet.

- Although Hong Kong is a Chinese territory, it operates fairly independently and does not require a visa for a U.S. citizen.

- The speed at which your visa is processed will depend on the current level of political tension.

- In general it's a pretty easy process to get a single entry tourist visa. If you don't live in a city where there is a Chinese consulate, use an expediting service.

- All visas take up a full page in your passport, so make sure you have enough pages for your trip.

Here's a little story to illuminate the process. Back in 2008, Rich was encouraged by his employer to become an Olympic torch bearer in Tibet. The process implied some vetting by the Chinese Olympic Committee, and with his employer's assistance Rich applied for the necessary visa.

Political tensions were very high at the time – Tibet was virtually sealed off from the outside world. There was no word back on the visa application, so Rich thought he'd never get to go. In fact, two days before his scheduled departure, the company's General Manager said it wasn't going to happen, and Rich cancelled his reservations.

Then, the following day, his visa was approved. He scrambled to rebook, and got on the plane as originally scheduled.

What happened? There's no way to know for sure, but Rich thinks a senior person with the company in Tibet vouched for him – he probably said there was no risk that Rich would turn his Olympic run into a "Free Tibet!" protest moment for the international media. Of course, had that been his intent, Rich would've risked arrest or at least the loss of his job.

Here's the kicker: It took 15 hours to fly from the East Coast to Beijing. Two days in Beijing to get the permit to enter Tibet. Five hours to fly from Beijing to Tibet's capital. A whole day in Tibet receiving instructions for the Olympic torch handoff and run. Three hours' waiting on a bus before the event.

And, the time actually running with the torch itself? Maybe 15 seconds. A sprint of perhaps 100 yards, albeit with a very full motorcade. Then backtracking through the whole travel process to get home!

BOOKING YOUR FLIGHT

- There are now many direct flights to major cities in China, both from U.S. carriers as well as multiple Chinese national airlines.

- Chinese airlines have a good safety record, and are flying new planes.

- For quality of service, U.S. airlines are typically judged as having an advantage.

- If you're a member of a frequent flier program with an American carrier, keep in mind that going to China and back will involve a lot of miles.

- As we noted earlier in the book, another reason to book a U.S. carrier is that they often get preferential take-off and landing rights at major airports since the Chinese want to appear efficient and modern. This can make a difference in a place like Beijing, which can be subject to sandstorms, air pollution and other visibility problems.

- If your trip is beginning or ending in southern China, consider going through Hong Kong. You'll have a greater choice of airlines and better quality of service.

- If your company is paying your way, and does not allow you to fly in business class, it's important to find out whether they will allow you to book the various forms of "coach- plus" seats. These seats have more leg room, which can really make a difference on a 15- hour flight.

- If you've never flown to Asia before, there's really no

way to prepare for the flight. It's a long time in the air and there's just no way around that. Heed the usual advice to get out of your seat regularly and moderate your alcohol intake.

- If you're traveling on business, always allow at least 24 hours on the ground in Asia before your first meeting. Remember that your hosts will not be suffering from jet lag, and you'll want to be fresh and alert, especially for your first meeting

CHOOSING A HOTEL

- Asia in general has the best quality hotels in the world. Because labor is so cheap, it's not a problem to get whatever level of service you want.

- Asia also has some of the worst hotels. For a Chinese working person who is not at a high level in a company, the standard room would be unacceptable to a western traveler. Think of a tiny space with a small uncomfortable bed, no amenities, an old bathroom, and mildew throughout.

- If you rely on hotel star ratings, make sure you check them carefully. A three-star Chinese-rated hotel is not the same as a three-star U.S. hotel.

- There are terrific bargains to be had at many high-quality luxury hotels. Surf the web for bargains.

- Breakfast at Chinese hotels is often included in the room price. You may be treated to a lavish buffet of international food – an omelet station, cold cuts and salads, cereal, fruit, juices, as well as ample Asian fare (warm soy milk with crullers, rice cereal, and dumplings). If you're on a limited budget, a big breakfast at a quality hotel can become your major meal of the day.

- Most hotels offer complimentary Wi-Fi. Remember, though, that China controls internet access within its borders, so all foreign websites may not be available.

- The Chinese smoke cigarettes – a lot. If you're sensitive to smoke, be sure to ask for a non-smoking room.

- If you plan to use your cell phone while traveling, check to see whether it will work and how much it will cost. You may need to sign up for a special temporary travel plan.

GIFTS

- Always prepare to take gifts along for your Chinese hosts. Your CFO may frown on it, but gift-giving is standard operating procedure in Asia.

- The bigger the brand, the better.

- You need to anticipate how many people will be in your meetings, and always want to acknowledge the lead person with a more important gift.

- You can't buy gifts when you get there. The Chinese will expect something from your home country.

- Depending on who you're meeting, the cost of the gift is not necessarily critical. Decorative stamps and small coin sets are perfectly fine (and easier to carry than a lot of other gift options).

- You can expect to always receive a friendship gift in your meetings.   If you don't, you need to question whether your meeting had any value

FOOD

- China has a full choice of foods available for travelers. On your leisure meals, you can get virtually anything from Pizza Hut and KFC to street food of barbequed insects dipped in hot oil for a crunchy treat.

- English is often not spoken at all in restaurants, but staff are usually very helpful to foreign tourists. You'll often see posted photos of various dishes, or you can point to a dish going by to indicate that you'd like to try it.

- Hotel restaurants – and specifically, the more expensive hotel restaurants – will offer the easiest experience for Westerners.   They have English speakers on hand to assist.

- If you're adventurous, you can have a novel experience by going into a new neighborhood and trying something different. Rich used to do this, and reports that he always had fun. Don't be insulted if they ask you to pay when you order. They don't see a lot of adventurous Westerners.

- Generally you don't tip for service.

- Remember that if you're invited to a banquet, it's probably in your honor. Be prepared to eat and drink freely. Remember, "I'm taking medicine" is your only out for not drinking.

- Practice using chopsticks before you leave home. At fancy restaurants, Westerners will be provided silverware, but you will always score extra points if you say, "thanks, but I use chopsticks."

- Remember that food, and the social act of communal dining, is especially important to the Chinese. It's where the deals happen.

- It's important to be seen as a generous business partner. You should always invite your hosts for a restaurant meal. If you're a new traveler, it's totally appropriate to ask them to pick a place and you'll pay. If you're there for a while, they'll probably take you out too.

SIGHTSEEING

- Often your hosts will make themselves available as guides, or arrange for others to guide you. They'll make sure you see the local sights.

- Showing an interest in the local culture will help to build your business relationships.

- The Chinese are very proud of their culture and history, and much more knowledgeable than Americans are about United States history.   Their knowledge goes all the way back to the early dynasties.

A FEW RANDOM POINTS THAT WE WANT TO STUFF IN

- You can't really do impromptu social events as a Western visitor in China.   Your schedule should be pretty well set by the time you arrive.

- In the West (and especially in the States) it's not unusual for colleagues of the opposite sex to hug or kiss each other on the cheek.   That doesn't happen in China, where a more formal code rules. You shake hands.

- Don't expect to lock down any major deals on your first visit, or expect impromptu follow up meetings while you're there.   If that does happen, it means you've got something of urgent value.

- When you get home, it's important to send a letter of thanks. Remember, you're building a relationship.

GANBEI! ...
AND (TRY TO) GO EASY ON THE RICE WINE!

RICHARD A. BRADSPIES

Is a 40-year veteran of international business. He spent 11 years as deputy general manager for the bank of china. He also worked for Dutch, French and German banks.

J. D. FOX

Is a manhattan-based writer and pr executive. His legal thriller, The Matriarchs, was published by Amazon in 2011.
He is an adjunct professor at New York University – teaching in a Master's program in which the majority of students come from China.

The authors met while volunteering at God's Love We Deliver, a non-religious charitable organization providing meals to New Yorkers with serious illnesses.

Their many conversations while chopping vegetables led to a "This Could Be a Book!" Moment, and here it is.